*Computer Graphics
and Applications*

Computer Graphics and Applications

DENNIS HARRIS
Polytechnic of North London

LONDON NEW YORK
Chapman and Hall

First published 1984 by Chapman and Hall Ltd
11 New Fetter Lane, London EC4P 4EE
Published in the USA
by Chapman and Hall
29 West 35th Street, New York NY 10001
Reprinted 1986

© 1984 Dennis Harris

Printed in Great Britain at the University Press, Cambridge

British Library Cataloguing in Publication Data

Harris, Dennis
    Computer graphics and applications.
    1. Computer graphics
    I. Title
    001.64'43   T385

    ISBN 0-412-25080-2
    ISBN 0-412-25090-X Pbk

Library of Congress Cataloging in Publication Data

Harris, Dennis, 1952—
    Computer graphics and applications.

    Bibliography: p.
    Includes index.
    1. Computer graphics.   I. Title.
    T385.H344 1984   001.64'43   84-4958
    ISBN 0-412-25080-2
    ISBN 0-412-25090-X (pbk.)

Contents

Preface

Graphics is defined by the *Oxford English Dictionary* as 'of drawing, painting, engraving, etching, etc.; vividly descriptive, lifelike; of diagrams and symbolic curves'. This definition is a useful starting point for any treatment of computer graphics. It includes much of what computer graphics can already do, and what it will be able to achieve, in the future. The key phrase from that definition is 'vividly descriptive'. Computers have for a long time been used to produce 'diagrams and symbolic curves', but they are now capable of painting lifelike pictures, or creating animated films of imaginary landscapes and the creatures to fill them. What is important to grasp is the almost limitless potential of this new technology. It is with an awareness of this tremendous scope that computer graphics has become more than just one exciting branch of computer technology. It has become the youngest and most energetic of the visual disciplines.

Traditionally computer graphics evolved as a means to interpret and display the numbers with which the modern world of computers has become inundated. Computers were programmed to convert large volumes of indigestible data into histograms, pie charts, graphs and bar charts. What was intrinsically different about this traditional method of displaying numeric information was the rapidity and accuracy with which it could be accomplished by computer. This straightforward type of usage grew throughout the 1950s, several computer systems being able to produce plots on teletypes and lineprinters. By the mid-50s the SAGE Air Defence System was using a light pen, but there was still no grasp of dynamic interaction until 1963 and the advent of Ivan Sutherland's 'Sketchpad'. The Sketchpad system was subtitled 'A Man–Machine Communication System', and its objective was communication by interaction. To this end it visualized a man sitting in front of a screen and dynamically interacting with the displayed graphics by means of a light pen and symbol menu. Once this idea was realized it did not take long for large-scale business to become interested; the only stumbling block for widespread expansion was the state of the hardware.

In the early 1960s the only available display device was the vector refresh cathode ray tube (CRT). This was a cathode ray tube in which an electron beam drew a picture on a screen as a collection of straight lines (or vectors). The phosphors on the screen meant that the picture lasted only a fraction of a second before fading, so the picture had to be continuously drawn at least 30 times per second to maintain a steady image. Hard copy of the contents of the screen was possible either by camera or by redrawing the picture line by line on an *X, Y* vector plotter. The drawback of refresh displays was that they were complicated, expensive and had severe limitations on the number of lines they could display and update because of the large memory requirements involved. Every line that went into a picture had to be stored inside the display so that the picture could be repeatedly redrawn. This disadvantage was solved later in the 60s with the direct view storage tube (DVST). Whereas the refresh display must cycle through some form of file containing the information for every line displayed on the screen the storage tube display needed no such display memory. The storage tube display incorporated a screen coated with long-persistence phosphors so that once an electron beam has traced a line on the screen it stays there and requires no further refreshing. This allowed the display of far more complicated diagrams than were possible with existing refresh systems.

By the close of the 60s there was a great expansion in commercial involvement in computer graphics. This was a spur to the next important development – the arrival of raster based displays and plotters. These were the results, in the early 70s, of the computer graphics industry looking to t.v. technology to provide a new type of graphic device which would be inexpensive, and for the first time exploit the full potential of colour. They were made possible by the falling price, and increasing power, of semiconductor memory. The image on a raster scan terminal is built up in a similar way to that of a standard t.v. tube. It is essentially a rectangular grid of dots (one dot is known as a picture element or pixel). The size of this grid is known as the resolution of the terminal. A common display resolution is 512 by 512. This gives 262 144 individual dots. The terminal must have sufficient memory to describe at least two values for every single dot (or picture element). That minimum of two values will only record whether the picture element is on or off. More sophisticated displays contain enough information to describe subtle shades of colour for each dot. Obviously memory requirements are critical and as memory becomes cheaper raster displays will be able to display greater colour ranges.

Unfortunately the diversity and acceleration of hardware innovation over the last 20 years has not provided a sound framework for parallel software development. From the early 1960s hardware manufacturers provided graphic software to drive their own products. This software normally consisted of a set of routines that would allow the user to draw lines, curves, dots, and perhaps some text, but only on that manufacturer's hardware. It was up to the users to write software to accomplish anything more useful. That process of writing software was always very much a case of re-inventing the wheel. Today the picture is changing. For several years there has been an abundance of graphic software available, much of it claiming to be 'machine-independent'. This is software which can, in theory, run on virtually any mainframe computer. Such software was generally written in Fortran to facilitate ease of machine portability. The philosophy underlying these large libraries of graphic routines was that they would contain two sections. One would handle the required graphic computations, the other would translate the results into codes that would be understood by the user's specific terminal. More recently many people involved in computer graphics have tried to agree on one international standard that would define how these large libraries of software should be written. This is discussed in Chapter 4.

The aim of this book is to introduce the reader to as much as possible of the whole spectrum of computer graphics. To this end each chapter will try to give an understanding of the basic concepts and terminology covered by that chapter. The first chapter will begin by describing the range of graphic devices and facilities currently available.

1

Hardware

Computer graphics hardware comes in many shapes, colours and sizes. Some devices (like film recorders) are still very costly and, therefore, still quite rare, but generally speaking the continuous fall in the price of memory has meant that many more graphic devices have become accessible to increasing numbers of people.

Figure 1.1 illustrates the stages and hardware involved in a typical applica-

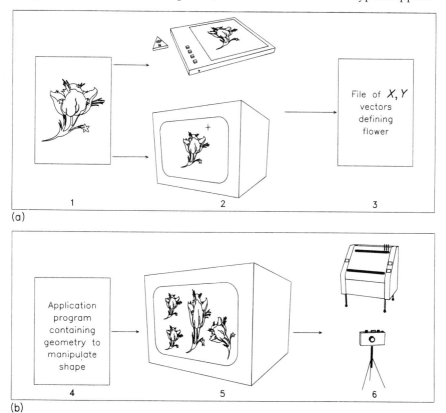

(a)

(b)

Fig. 1.1 (a) Creation and storage of a shape; (b) manipulation, display and output of shape.

tion for computer graphics — pattern design. In this example the shape of a flower is being put into a computer so that it can be modified interactively. In this particular case the flower is to be the basic component for a large textile design. The computer will be used to stretch and rotate the shape, and then to repeat the modified flower in a regular pattern to create an overall picture. If the display device is capable of colour it can then be used to try out various colour combinations. The hardware illustrated in this example embraces the three main categories of graphic hardware which are examined in this chapter:

A. Input devices. The original sketch of the flower is going to be digitized, that is, literally turned into numbers. Several different types of input tool exist to do this: mostly they convert a 2-D drawing or a 3-D object into X, Y or X, Y, Z coordinates. These coordinates are then stored on tape, disc, or some other medium.

B. Interactive devices. These are devices which can display a picture and allow it to be added to or changed in some way. In this example the flower might be stretched, rotated, or moved around the display screen. These three operations represent the geometrical manipulations of scaling, rotation and translation which are basic to much of computer graphics. This type of manipulation is normally computed by software, but these sorts of task are increasingly being performed by hardware inside the display devices themselves.

C. Output devices. When some satisfactory stage in the development of a picture has been arrived at there are two principal methods of producing hard copy output (i.e. something you can take away and look at). One is to send it to some form of plotter (normal for monochrome images), or, if it is a coloured-in image, to commit it to film or a colour plotter. In this chapter output devices are, for convenience, split into two sections: plotters and colour reproducers.

The stages illustrated are:

1. Original shape — may be picture or still in programmer's head.
2. Put shape into computer by digitizing or drawing interactively.
3. Shape stored as a series of vectors (or polygons, etc.)
4. Software to perform manipulations on file of vectors.
5. Display device showing translation, scaling and rotation.
6. Final picture output to film or paper.

1.1 INPUT DEVICES

Graphic input devices are necessary for two main reasons: to put into the computer pictorial data; and to aid in the manipulation of these data. They are often combined with software to facilitate these two functions. The five most common input tools are:

1. Tablet.
2. Joystick.
3. Mouse.
4. Light pen.
5. Trackball.

1.1.1 Graphic tablet

There are several variations of the graphic tablet (or digitizer). The basic type consists of an even surface containing a series of parallel wires in the X and Y directions. Conceptually it is very similar to a piece of graph paper. Some sort of stylus connected to the tablet can detect an individual X, Y coordinate by the signal at any given wire intersection. The analogue signals received from the stylus are processed by decoding logic to produce digital X, Y positions of the stylus. These coordinates are normally absolute from a user defined origin on the tablet. Usually the stylus does not have to be in contact with the tablet and often need only be within 2 cm of the surface. The stylus (which may be in the form of a pen or tracking cross) can be used to trace an existing diagram or create a new freehand picture. Software is useful to help in the definition of arcs, curves, repeated shapes, etc. Figure 1.2 illustrates a simple digitizer on which a picture of a flower has been placed ready for digitization.

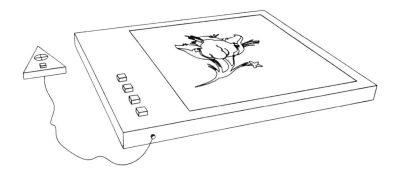

Fig. 1.2 Hi-pad digitizer

1.1.2 Joystick

The joystick found on graphic displays is a variation of the type found in aircraft. It is a stick that can be moved to the left or right, up or down. Two potentiometers (normally arranged at right angles to each other) sense the movement of the joystick and convert this into X, Y positions. This makes the joystick an ideal tool to control a cursor on a screen. In addition, by monitoring the degree to which the joystick is moved, the speed at which the cursor moves can be directly linked to the joystick. A drawback of this is that small, precise movements and positioning are very difficult to judge.

1.1.3 Mouse

The mouse consists of a small box on wheels which can be moved around by hand easily and quickly. On the bottom of the mouse two wheels set at right angles to each other drive potentiometers that are decoded to give relative movements. This makes the mouse, like the joystick, ideal to control a cursor. It is used, therefore, not to enter graphic data, but to interact with a program. To aid this usage it normally has a set of buttons on its top which can be programmed by software. In the example in Fig. 1.3 the buttons could be programmed to perform a manipulation on one of the menu-shapes.

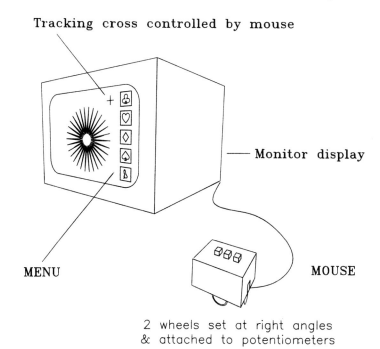

Fig. 1.3 Mouse

1.1.4 Light pen

The light pen is used primarily on vector refresh displays. It is a small, hand-held device which can detect the presence of light on a screen through a photocell within its barrel or tip. When the photocell senses light the activity of the display processor inside the display device is interrupted and the coordinates of the point on the screen can be returned to the user's program. This action is accomplished by a user pointing the light pen at a desired screen location and depressing a mechanical switch on the barrel of the pen or by pushing a retractable tip on the nose of the pen gently against the screen. Usually at this moment some application software will take over and perform an appropriate function such as drawing or erasing a line. The main disadvantage of the light pen is that it needs to be held up to the screen — which is very tiring.

1.1.5 Trackball

The trackball is a rotating ball in a socket which turns potentiometers to produce digital coordinates. It controls a screen cursor in direct proportion to the speed at which it is rolled and in the direction of its rotation. It is difficult to make large or rapid movements but it allows precise positioning of the cursor because of the easily controlled speed of rotation. Figure 1.4 illustrates a typical trackball. It is found often in aviation (radar operation, air-traffic control) and can be found on many video games.

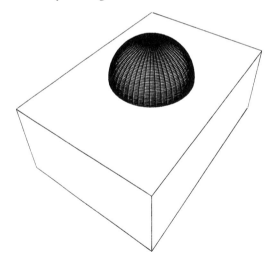

Fig. 1.4 Trackball

1.2 OUTPUT DEVICES

An output device is a piece of machinery that produces hard copy of a visual image on either paper or film. In computer graphics it is mostly a case of reproducing a diagram on a graph plotter or recording a highly coloured image from a t.v. type display on to some kind of permanent medium. Section 1.2.4 deals with full colour output. This section will look at graph plotters which come in three basic types:

1. Drum plotters.
2. Flat-bed plotters.
3. Electrostatic plotters.

1.2.1 Drum plotters

Drum plotters are probably the most widely known type of plotter and are usually found attached to mainframe computers. They are capable of producing very large, complex and multi-coloured diagrams. Figure 1.5 shows a Benson drum plotter. It has three pen holders which are supported above a drum. The pens may move along the length of this drum. Paper is wrapped around this drum which is rotated under the pens. Two stepping motors are used to drive the pens and the drum. A typical drum plotter speed is about 40 cm/s. In the early days of plotters the host computer had to compute every coordinate that went into defining one straight line. Today most plotters have at least enough intelligence to compute all the intermediate points between the start and end of a line, and many have built-in hardware to take as much computation away from the host as possible. Graphic functions such as generating arcs, drawing broken lines, and producing complex fonts are increasingly being relegated to microprocessors inside plotters. More advanced plotters allow the use of high-

Fig. 1.5 Benson 1322 drum plotter

level real-time languages such as Coral-66, and several types implement the facility to remember, and reproduce anywhere, entire pictures. This is extremely useful when a complex drawing contains many repetitions of a basic component such as a circuit.

1.2.2 Flat-bed plotters

Flat-bed plotters fall into two categories: small desk-top plotters (A4 or A3 size) and large table plotters up to 4 m by 2 m. Both operate on the same principle. A pen is supported on a gantry. The pen can move along the gantry (*Y* movement) and the gantry itself can move along the flat bed (*X* movement). The driving mechanism is usually either stepping motors or DC servo motors. A typical speed may be 25 cm/s. Although flat-bed plotters are usually slower and less accurate than drum plotters they offer several useful features:

1. They can generally accept any kind of paper, including plastic film, for over-head projection.
2. Pens can be wet ink, liquid ink ball, ballpoint, fibre-tip or even brush tip.
3. They can more easily accommodate several pens. The Calcomp 81 is a recent, inexpensive flat-bed plotter which has eight pen holders. As a rule drum plotters don't go beyond four pen holders.
4. Some can be used as digitizers.

Figure 1.6 shows a Hewlett Packard flat-bed plotter. The particular model illustrated is a high-resolution A3 plotter. Besides acting normally as an output device this plotter can also act as an input device (a digitizer) by inserting a

This gantry can move
across the plotter

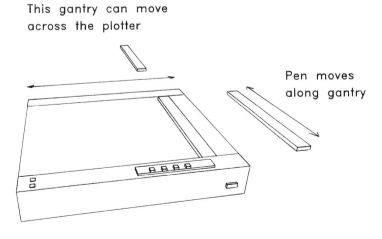

Pen moves
along gantry

Fig. 1.6 Flat-bed plotter

fibre-optic pen into one of its pen holders. This pen can then be moved under manual control until it is directly over a desired point when a button on the panel can be pushed. The plotter will then send that X, Y coordinate to the host computer. Although a reasonably accurate method of digitizing, it is very slow and awkward.

1.2.3 Electrostatic plotters

Electrostatic plotters are comparatively recent. They produce an image on paper in the same way as a t.v. set produces an image, by displaying dots. Figure 1.7 demonstrates the basic technique. As paper passes through the plotter a row of electrodes deposit charges on chemically treated paper. These electrodes are really a series of recording heads and the resolution of the plotter is determined by the density, spacing and size of the addressable electrodes. Once the electrical nibs have deposited a charge the paper passes through a toner bath which develops the plot by adhering black toner to the charged areas. The paper then goes to a drier. The entire process is not unlike a Xerox copier.

A common resolution for such plotters is about 80 dots/cm. At this resolution they are good for quick checking but not good enough for high-quality engineering or architectural drawings. However, the fact that they are able to provide complex plots very rapidly makes them an increasingly popular output device. Their disadvantages are that they are usually only available in black, they have limited resolution, and they require extensive manipulation of the plotting data. This manipulation of the data is necessary because the paper (unlike the drum plotter) can only move in one direction. This means the entire picture to be drawn must be sorted into a linear plotting sequence and the vectors turned into a digital raster dot format. This would be extremely time consuming for a host processor and so the vector-to-raster conversion is normally performed by the electrostatic processor.

1.2.4. Colour output devices

Several types of output device are geared to producing coloured hard copy images:

1. Camera systems.
2. Matrix printers.
3. Ink-jet plotters.
4. Film recorders.

(a) Camera systems

It is cheap and easy to aim an everyday camera at a visual display and take a photograph. Often this is the only economic way to try to record a coloured

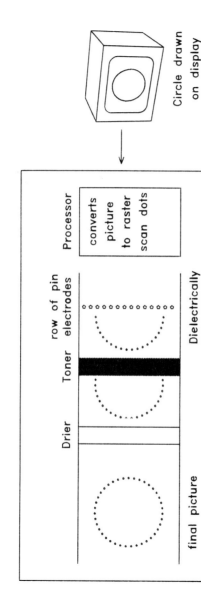

Circle drawn on display

Processor

converts picture to raster scan dots

row of pin electrodes

Toner

Drier

Dielectrically coated paper

final picture

Fig. 1.7 Electrostatic plotter

image. Slightly more sophistication is possible by using a special Polaroid camera with a monitor hood, and it is possible to purchase a high-quality 35 mm or large format camera and use it together with professional colour-corrected film. There are two main disadvantages: it is virtually impossible for cameras to capture the colours on a visual display and it is extremely difficult to avoid edge distortion on an off-the-screen photograph because of the curvature of monitor screens.

Video signal camera systems overcome these problems by connecting directly into the RGB output of the raster display. Each of the three colour signals is individually displayed on a high-quality flat-screen monochrome monitor within the camera system itself. This monochrome monitor is photographed three times with an appropriately coloured filter in front of it for each colour signal being displayed. By superimposing all three pictures together a full colour print is produced. Because these systems produce hard copy generated directly by the video signal they can actually produce prints higher in quality than the video display itself. Their one overriding drawback is cost. The systems that produce 8 x 10″ prints (e.g. Calcomp Camera System) cost as much as a good quality colour terminal and each print is very expensive. More economic, though less versatile, systems are becoming available. These are geared towards generating 35 mm prints and slides.

(b) Matrix printers

Matrix printers are easily modified to produce colour plots by using three or four colour ribbons. In a three-ribbon printer three passes are made over the paper (this can be line by line or page by page). On the first pass all the yellow data are plotted (ribbon colours are normally yellow, magenta and cyan because they use dyes not light). The paper is wound back to the start, a second pass is made in magenta, and the process is repeated for the cyan data. By inter-spersing dots of the three available colours in varying densities larger ranges of colours are possible. Two examples of matrix plotters are the Integrex CX80 colour matrix printer and the Trilog Colourplot C-100. The CX80 can produce seven colours but is of limited resolution. The Trilog C-100 is more versatile and has a resolution of 100 dots/in. The main advantage of matrix colour printers is that they are fast and cheap. Their main drawbacks are that they are noisy and cannot produce smoothly coloured in areas.

(c) Ink-jet plotters

Ink-jet plotters form an image by depositing fine ink droplets on paper. Several types exist but generally they consist of three major elements:

1. A print head containing three ink-jets (normally magenta, cyan and yellow).
2. A rotating drum to hold the output (paper or acetate).

3. Some microprocessor system to control the deflection of very fine ink drop-lets to the paper.

The ink-jets produce a constant-size image element that can vary from 1 to 5 points/mm. A sophisticated plotter like the Applicon ink-jet plotter (Plates 1 and 2 were produced on this plotter) has a resolution of about 50 points/cm. Each element may contain no colour, a single colour, or any combination of the three coloured jets for a total of six colour combinations plus black and white. Software can be used to define matrices of picture elements which vary the number of filled elements to achieve several thousand shades of colour.

Ink-jet plotters provide high-quality shaded pictures and have the added advantage of being very fast. This is mostly due to the fact that they do not have to make several passes (as with the matrix printer), each coloured element of an image being simultaneously produced. Several makes are now commercially available and they are gaining increasing popularity.

(d) Film recorders

Film recorders produce images on some type of photographic film. There are two main methods of forming the images, one by using a CRT to display the image, which is then photographed with a camera, and second, using an elec-tron beam or laser beam to write directly on to special film. The incoming graphic data control the CRT or writing device.

Two examples of film recorders are the FR80 (resolution 4000×6000) and the Calcomp 1670 (resolution 16384×16384). Both can produce output on 16 mm or 35 mm film. Typically, film recorders are possessed by large bureaux or central institutions since they are extremely expensive. They are high-quality devices so are generally used only for finished plots (i.e. a graphic designer might construct a picture on a medium resolution raster display and, once satisfied with a picture, then send that plot to the film recorder). They also have the advantage of writing on film extremely fast.

1.3 INTERACTIVE DEVICES

In the 1960s and 70s direct-view displays relied almost exclusively on CRT tech-nology. There were two types of CRT display — random scan and raster scan. Random scan CRTs trace out on a screen only those vectors generated by a program. A raster scan CRT illuminates a series of spots which form an image in a similar way to a t.v. set. Figure 1.8 illustrates the two types of CRT displaying the same six-sided figure. This section will deal with the various types of random scan and raster scan CRT and will close with a very brief examination of the technology that is developing quietly but rapidly — flat panel displays.

There are five main types of direct-view display:

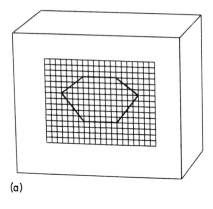
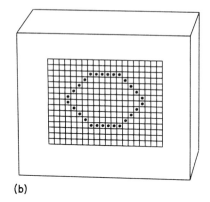

Fig. 1.8 (a) Random scan; (b) raster scan

1. Direct-view storage tubes.
2. Refresh (calligraphic displays).
3. Raster scan systems.
4. Flat panel displays.
5. 3-D displays.

1.3.1 Direct-view storage tubes

Direct-view storage tubes were first developed to examine images that did not require rapid updating. This included architectural plans, waveforms, circuits, etc. This was a direct consequence of the nature of the display which produces a steady, flicker-free picture. The graphic image is coated on the screen itself as a semi-permanent drawing. The method is illustrated in Fig. 1.9.

The direct view storage tube uses a CRT that is controlled electrostatically. The main electron gun emits a tightly focused (writing) beam at the storage grid (a fine wire mesh situated immediately behind the viewing screen). This results in the storage grid losing more electrons than it gains in those areas where the writing beam strikes it. Hence a positive charge pattern is generated, corresponding to the track of the writing beam. At this stage a second electron gun (flood gun) emits a broad, low-energy electron beam. The positively charged areas accelerate the flood gun electrons though the grid mesh, causing the illumination of the long-persistence phosphor on the viewing screen in correspondence to the charge patterns on the storage grid. The viewing screen is at high potential (about 10 kV) to accelerate electrons through the storage grid.

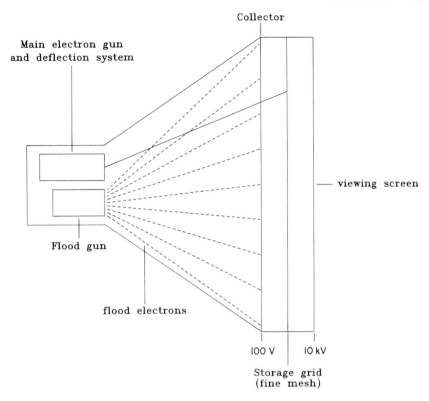

Fig. 1.9 Direct-view storage tube

(a) Advantages

1. The direct-view storage tube easily doubles as an ordinary v.d.u.
2. It provides a steady flicker-free image even when displaying very large amounts of data.
3. It offers very high resolution.
4. It is relatively cheap.
5. It is driven by ordinary ASCII codes.

(b) Disadvantages

1. It is very difficult to selectively erase part of the image. To change part of the picture necessitates clearing the screen and redrawing the entire picture.
2. There is low brightness (or value contrast).
3. No grey levels are possible.

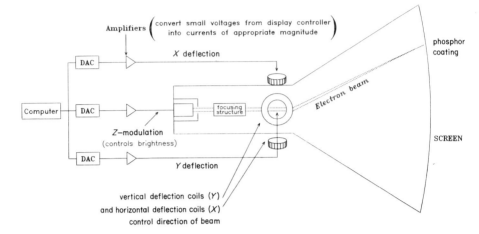

Fig. 1.10 Cathode ray tube

4. There is no colour capability.
5. It cannot use a light pen.

   True interactive graphics requires some form of selective erasure and picture manipulation. Some strides have been made in this direction, for instance a partial refresh technique as used on the Tektronix 4081 allows the last few actions entered to be drawn in a non-stored manner and only directly stored after verification. However, for animation and sophisticated interaction it is necessary to look to other types of display.

1.3.2 Vector refresh displays

The vector refresh display does not use a long-persistence phosphor but instead utilizes short-persistence phosphors to allow interaction and animation. Figure 1.10 demonstrates the method by which a digital piece of information generated by the computer is finally realized on the screen of a normal CRT:

1. The computer produces X, Y coordinates in digital form.
2. Digital-to-analogue (DAC) convertors change digital information into analogue form.
3. Amplifiers convert analogue voltages into currents of appropriate magnitude.
4. The electron beam is moved on the screen to a point proportional to the currents fed into the X, Y deflection coils.

Further control is possible by a third DAC (Z-modulation) which can control the level of brightness of the electron beam.

Once the electron beam strikes a phosphor it is excited and glows for a very short period. To maintain a steady image the picture must be re-drawn before the phosphor glow fades completely. This requires information to be repeatedly transferred to the display, sufficiently quickly to avoid any flicker. Generally, with normal short-persistence phosphors this means refreshing the image between 30 and 50 times/s. It would be too demanding to expect the computer to re-generate an entire image so frequently. Therefore virtually all refresh displays contain a display processor between the computer and the CRT itself. This display processor accesses a stored description of a picture (called a display file) to refresh the screen. If this display file is too complex the picture cannot be drawn in the required time, resulting in flicker. With modern displays it is possible to draw in excess of 100 000 vectors within the rate required to maintain a flicker-free picture. Display files may be modified dynamically by the computer to allow selective erasure and animation. Usualy the display file is held in memory local to the display system to reduce the load on the CPU.

A display file usually contains two classes of instruction:

1. Drawing instructions.
2. Control instructions.

(i) Drawing instructions
1. Point plotting: to define an absolute coordinate.
2. Vector plotting: normally one incremental X, Y coordinate, the starting point having previously been defined by a point instruction.
3. Text generation: text can be drawn as a series of vectors where each character is held as a separate subroutine. Alternatively there may be a hardware character generator where each character is encoded in a data field (typically in a single 8-bit byte).
4. Brightness: this might also include blinking or line style.

(ii) Control instructions
This consists mainly of jump instructions. The most important jump instruction is the subroutine jump. This enables sections of code to be called repeatedly. Other control instructions include loading transformation matrices so that subsequently drawn coordinates will be transformed before being displayed. When the complete picture has been drawn, a jump instruction returns control to the beginning of the display file, thus initiating the refresh cycle.

(a) Advantages of refresh vector displays

1. They offer high resolution.
2. They allow a high degree of interaction (light pen, etc.).
3. They can allow varying levels of intensity.
4. Selective erasure is possible.

5. There is a high transformation capability: rotation, scaling, translation, perspectives, etc. are relatively straightforward. These facilities are often implemented in the display hardware.

(b) Disadvantages

1. They are usually very expensive.
2. It is difficult to avoid flicker with complex pictures.
3. There is very little colour capability.
4. Realistic images are very difficult to generate.

Refresh displays are good for applications where interaction is desirable, especially where dynamically changing lines are required (e.g. computer-aided design). They are most commonly used in expensive systems where they can offer variable brightness and high resolution. Their chief problem lies in the manipulation of complex images. To overcome this problem many systems (e.g. the Vector General 3000 series) incorporate hardware transformation, line textures, arc generation, scaling and rotation, and font generation.

(c) Beam-penetration colour CRTs

Although vector refresh displays are normally monochrome there are several colour CRTs available which use beam penetration to produce coloured images. These displays are restricted in performance because of limitations on the phosphors used. Some computer generated image (CGI) systems incorporate colour CRTs for high performance requirements. The CRTs basically consist of two coatings of red and green phosphors on the inside of the display screen. The strength of the electron beam can be controlled to achieve different penetrations into these phosphors and hence the colour of the resultant image can be controlled.

There are several drawbacks to beam-penetration systems. Very few colours are selectable (usually only red, green, orange and yellow), blue in particular being extremely difficult to generate. The brightness of the display is relatively low, and it is very complex to display a large number of flicker-free lines because of the necessity of switching the potentials on the beam-accelerating circuitry at very high speeds.

1.3.3 Raster scan displays

Storage tube and vector refresh systems were for more than a decade the only display devices available to the computer. Neither was cheap or very widely used and it became apparent by the late 1960s that there was a need for some other type of device. The obvious choice seemed to be somehow to make use of

starting point of first scan

Horizontal scan restarts again

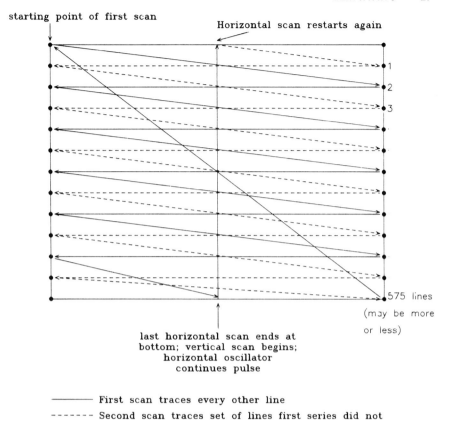

last horizontal scan ends at
bottom; vertical scan begins;
horizontal oscillator
continues pulse

575 lines

(may be more
or less)

1
2
3

——————— First scan traces every other line

- - - - - - Second scan traces set of lines first series did not

Fig. 1.11 Raster scanning

t.v. technology to utilize t.v. systems as display devices for computers. The modern raster scan display is the result of that work.

Figure 1.11 shows the method by which a t.v. CRT builds up a t.v. image. A broadcasting station sends a signal containing special synchronizing pulses. Circuits in the t.v. use the 'sync' pulses to get in step with the transmitted signal. There are horizontal sync pulses to start the horizontal sweep of beam and vertical pulses to start the vertical trace of beam. In between these sync pulses is the video information that makes up a single horizontal line on the display screen. In a t.v. tube that supports 575 lines of picture information there would be 768 dots on each horizontal scan line. This would result in a 4:3 aspect ratio.

To translate this t.v. system into a computer—device relationship the display screen is divided into a matrix or 'raster' of dots (512 by 512 is a very common

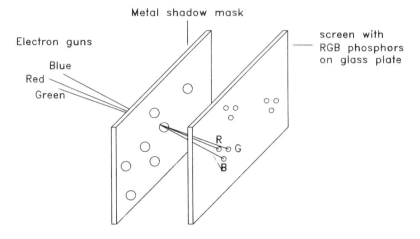

Fig. 1.12 Shadow-mask colour CRT

size for raster displays). The individual dots are known as pixels (short for 'pic-ture elements'). The computer must somewhere store information for each individual pixel. This information at its simplest would be contained by 1 bit per pixel giving either black or white. Intensity levels or colour require several bits of information per pixel. Colour is achieved by driving the red, green and blue guns of a cathode tube separately. 1 bit per pixel per gun (i.e. 3 bits per pixel) gives eight colours. Each bit defining one pixel can be considered as a separate memory plane. The early raster scan systems had only 1 bit per pixel; many systems today have up to 24 bits (or planes) per pixel giving over 16 million colour combinations (e.g. AED 512, Genisco GCT-3000). In the hardware every pixel is usually an image of one word in some form of semiconductor (typically MOS) memory. A scanner is used to continually translate the contents of this semiconductor memory into a t.v. signal for the display monitor.

A raster scan display produces colour output which must be fed to some sort of monitor. The most common type is the shadow-mask CRT found in the majority of domestic colour t.v. sets. Figure 1.12 illustrates the main principle of this device. The electron beams from three guns (red, green and blue) are directed at a metal mask which dictates the areas of phosphor on the screen to be hit by the beams. Only about a quarter of the beam goes through the mask to hit the triangles of phosphor on the screen. Each colour beam hits its respective phosphor colour on the screen, the mask shadows this beam from the other colour phosphors. This results in a brighter and more controllable image than the beam-penetration tube, and allows a very large number of colours to be generated.

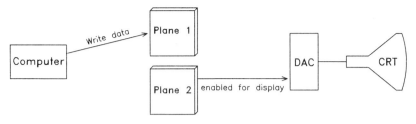

Display plane 2 only,
write new data to plane 1

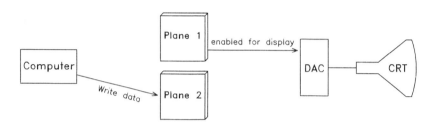

Now display plane 1 only and
update information in plane 2

Fig. 1.13 Pixel plane selection

(a) Pixel plane animation

Simple animation on colour terminals is possible by writing different picture data
to individual pixel planes and displaying these planes one by one. Figure 1.13
shows this process in action on a two-plane colour terminal. As plane 1 is selected
for display the picture data in plane 2 is changed. Plane 2 is then displayed while
the picture data in plane 1 is updated. As long as the computer controlling the
terminal can generate a new image in each pixel plane rapidly enough then this
technique produces quite reasonable animation. Alternatively several views of an
object (e.g. a molecule) can be written to a number of planes and then by
sequentially selecting these planes for display the object can be made to 'rock' to
and fro.

(b) Look-up tables

In a colour terminal the number of pixel planes determines the maximum value of each pixel. If a terminal had four planes this value would be between 0000 and 1111 (0 to 15). It is common practice to use this value as an index into a look-up table (LUT). This table is a separate, much smaller piece of memory that contains a 'palette' of colours. Whereas a pixel plane has to contain one bit of memory for every pixel on the terminal, the LUT need only contain sufficient memory to specify (in this example) sixteen colours. These colours can be very fine shades. For instance, in a four plane terminal it is normal to allow the LUT to define any of 4096 colours (four bits for each of the red, green and blue phosphors). This terminal would then be able to display any 16 colours from a palette of 4096. This technique is used to reduce the amount of memory (which means money) required to display multiple colours. To show 4096 colours simultaneously on a terminal would require 12 bits of memory for every pixel. Look-up tables have the advantage of enabling animation (see p. 135).

(c) Disadvantages

1. Resolution is more limited than with random scan displays mainly because of memory requirements and the complexity of monitor circuitry.
2. Geometric transformations in hardware are possible but very difficult. Some systems can accomplish full picture scaling, translation and rotation in real time.
3. Aliasing is a big problem. Straight lines not purely vertical or horizontal exhibit a 'staircasing' effect because of limitations in resolution. Software anti-aliasing is heavy on processor time. Some systems do now feature hardware anti-aliasing.
4. Selective erase is achieved with considerable difficulty. Normally redrawing a line or dot in the background colour constitutes an erasing action.
5. Animation: only advanced systems can load the video store (containing all the pixel information) rapidly enough to approach real-time animation.

(d) Advantages

1. Raster scan displays are still frequently used to simulate random scan displays.
2. Polygons can be filled in colour very rapidly.
3. Extremely complex images can be displayed without flicker.
4. Raster scan displays make increasing use of t.v. technology for sophisticated manipulation of the image (e.g. mixing t.v. pictures with computer-generated images).
5. Photographic realism is possible using colour-shaded polygons for texture and illumination effects.

Vector displays were originally implemented for engineering applications and are excellent for displaying high resolution black-and-white line drawings. Raster devices were invented for more general purposes and are more easily adaptable to the needs of realism. Some areas of usage are:

1. Flight and tanker simulation: Marconi Radar, Rediffusion for instance.
2. Animation: used by Walt Disney, New York Institute of Technology and Halas and Bachelor for cartoon animation, and by biologists, engineers, physicists, chemists for scientific animation.
3. Design and illustration: for machine parts, integrated circuit design, technical illustrations.

1.3.4 Flat panel displays

In the last few years a great deal of time, energy and money has been devoted to the new flat panel display technologies. The attraction of these devices is apparent in the popularity of the millions of watch and pocket computer displays that have been available for several years. The small alphanumeric displays that these feature are dominated by flat panel systems but there are several obstacles in implementing this technology to large volume displays. In particular there is no imminent likelihood of colour CRTs being replaced by the wave of electronic devices in current development. A conventional shadow-mask CRT can display any colour, is robust, and is reasonably simple to drive. For a flat panel display to seriously compete the primary problem to overcome is not really producing the display itself — several sophisticated prototypes have already been demonstrated — but in driving such a large panel quickly, cheaply and efficiently. In this situation the only safe prediction to make is that the day of the flat panel display in computer graphics may be distant, but is almost certainly inevitable.

Flat panel displays can be broken down into two simple categories — active and passive. An active type is so called because it emits light by the conversion of electrical energy. A passive type modulates light which is either natural light reflected off the display itself, or transmitted light. The main types are:

1. Active: light-emitting diodes (LED); electroluminescent; gas discharge.
2. Passive: liquid crystal (LCD); electrochromic.

(a) Light-emitting diodes

The LED is used very widely in simple alphanumeric displays. In these they are configured as seven-segment characters. Although for many years only red light emission diodes have been available they are now produced in the yellow, green and orange regions of the spectrum. Their main advantages are that they are very bright, reliable and economic. The main disadvantage is that they are not suited to large area displays (although 200 × 200 displays are manufactured) because each element of the display has to be made up from individual chips. This limits their usefulness to displays of two or four rows of alphanumeric information.

(b) Electroluminescent displays

One of the most promising contenders for large scale flat displays is, conversely, based on technology well known since the 1940s. Electroluminescent displays work by phosphors emitting light in electrical fields. Phosphor powder, or more recently a thin film of phosphor, is placed between two plates of electrodes. The two plates of electrodes act as an X-axis and a Y-axis for addressing the phosphors. In the latest systems the thin layers of phosphor film are transparent and a black layer is placed behind the film to improve the contrast. The two current drawbacks of these systems are that the brightness of the display is quite low, and their longevity is still very questionable. Their advantage is that they are rugged and can be multiplexed to create a large scale display. A 512 × 640 colour version is already under development.

(c) Gas discharge displays

These devices are known variously as photoluminescent, gas-discharge, gas plasma and plasma panel displays. Figure 1.14 shows the plasma panel display.

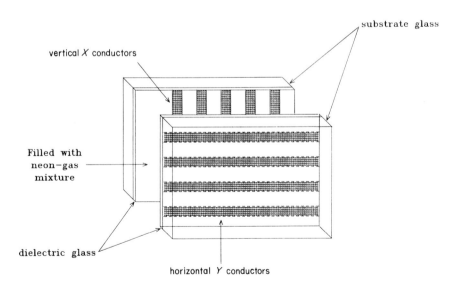

Fig. 1.14 Plasma panel

It consists of two outer layers of glass carrying transparent conducting strips one layer in the X direction and one layer in the Y direction. Gold electrodes are deposited on these plates. There are typically 512 electrodes in each direction, arranged to form a grid of intersections. When a voltage is applied to specific X, Y electrodes then at that intersection the neon gas between the plates will ionize and produce a plasma glow. The voltage can then be reduced to a small regular pulse to sustain a clear, steady picture. To turn off the electrodes it is necessary to reduce the voltage to the X, Y electrodes to a level less than the regular pulse voltage. This makes the plasma panel very similar to the storage tube (with no need for refresh memory), except that it allows a degree of selective erasure. In fact the plasma panel is not widely used in computer graphics due to its low resolution (commonly about 25 electrodes/cm) but is more often found as a special purpose alphanumeric display. Though there are some large format plasma panels currently available.

(d) Disadvantages

1. Limited resolution.
2. Monochrome — only allows single intensity.
3. Complex addressing and wiring requirements.
4. Low level of brightness.
5. Relatively expensive.

(e) Advantages

1. Flat screen.
2. Allows selective writing and erasure.
3. Screen can be used for back-screen projection.

All that remains to be said here is that a great deal of research is going into sophisticated multiplexing of these panels to achieve good quality coloured images and high resolution. A prototype produced in Japan has shown the possibilities of this.

The main problems to conquer before such displays could rival CRTs are the high cost of such displays and the present low levels of brightness. One useful advantage of gas plasma panels is that they can be used in conjunction with projected images. The glass panel is almost totally transparent, allowing back projectors to superimpose images with the actual displayed image.

(f) Electrochromic displays

Electrochromic displays work by applying voltages to specially treated electro-lytic cells to produce a change in the state of an electrode. In the cell an electrode is coated with a layer of tungsten oxide; changing the voltage to the cell changes the state of this electrode. Normally the tungsten oxide layer is coated to the surface of a transparent cathode so that an appropriate voltage will turn the normally clear tungsten oxide blue. The advantages of these types of display are that they are clearly visible from wide viewing angles, have very low power consumption (less than 5 V), have memory and are cheap to produce. Unfortunately the change in state takes 0.5 s and this, coupled with difficulties in addressing rows of them quickly, means that they are likely to be limited to simple one line displays.

(g) Liquid crystal

Some organic liquids are composed of molecules which form elongated crystals. These crystals can flow like liquids and possess very useful optical properties. Electrical fields can be manipulated to switch the crystals from a transparent to an opaque state or vice versa. One of the most common methods of controlling this switching is the twisted-nematic display. In this type the liquid crystal lies between two glass electrodes (see Fig. 1.15) and the molecules are aligned so that their orientation differs by right angles on the surface of the crystal cell. In this state light can pass through. Applying a small electrical field reorients the molecules and prevents the passage of light.

Liquid crystal displays have several drawbacks. Switching speeds are slow giving poor response, multiplexing is difficult resulting in poor contrast, and the driving circuitry is relatively expensive. There are also definite advantages. The current required for switching is very small, the advent of new dichroic dyes will allow much improved colour, and the use of large silicon slices will greatly ease the problem of multiplexing. There is a good chance that fairly high resolution colour graphics will be available soon using LCD technology.

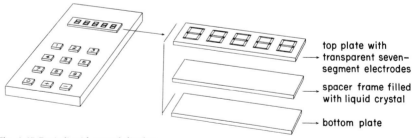

top plate with transparent seven-segment electrodes

spacer frame filled with liquid crystal

bottom plate

Fig. 1.15 Basic liquid crystal display

1.3.5 Mirror displays

For many years users in a wide number of application areas have been searching for more effective means of displaying 3-D images than have been

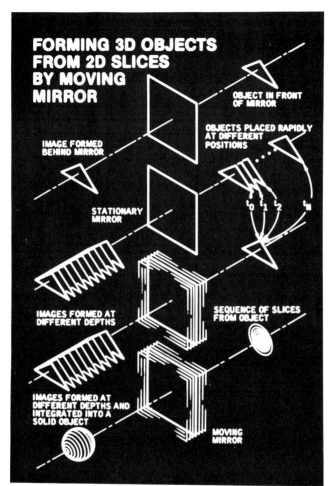

Fig. 1.16 (Courtesy Genisco Computers Corporation)

available. The most well-known and popular method has been to generate a stereo pair of pictures on to a conventional graphic v.d.u. This method requires generating two images of an object from two slightly different viewpoints. Once the pair is displayed then it can be viewed through special spectacles which fuse the pair into a 3-D image (Molecular modelling systems in particular use this technique). However, it suffers from two major defects. First, it is often very difficult, and invariably very tiring, to focus the eyes on such stereo images. Second, it doesn't produce a real image which, once generated, can be looked at from different angles. This situation has led to a large amount of activity to find

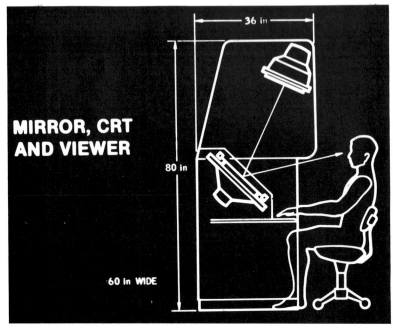

Fig. 1.17 (Courtesy Genisco Computers Corporation)

some display system that overcomes these problems. Most of this activity has centred on two very different solutions. One is to use the computer to generate and control holographic images. This requires a great deal of computer processing plus very specialized and costly equipment. The second approach has been pioneered by Genisco Computers. It hinges on the use of a rapidly oscillating mirror to produce an image not on a screen but in real space. Genisco have now marketed a complete system using this technology.

Figure 1.16 demonstrates the basic principles of the Genisco mirror display. An image is first built up on a high speed CRT. The user looks not at this but at a vibrating mirror which interprets the picture on the CRT (illustrated in Fig. 1.17). The mirror is constructed so that it can be rapidly vibrated by a hifi woofer connected to it. The image of each point on the CRT has not only an (X, Y) coordinate, as apparent on the flat screen, but also a Z coordinate. The mirror is vibrated in synchronization with the depth of the point displayed on the CRT so that a bright spot is formed (with a true X, Y, Z location) in a real volume of space. In the Genisco display this 'image volume' is 20 cm × 25 cm × 30 cm. The depth of this volume (30 cm) is divided into 46,000 possible Z coordinates, each of which can be thought of as a plane. Figure 1.16 shows a sphere composed of slices. Figure 1.18 is a photograph of an image produced on this display.

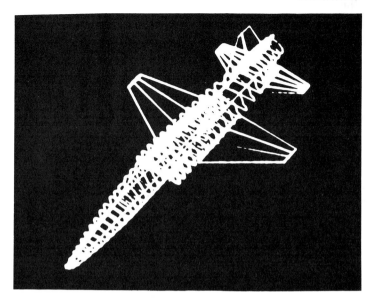

Fig. 1.18 (Courtesy Genisco Computers Corporation)

The vibrating mirror display system has obvious advantages over conventional terminals in displaying 3-D data. It allows a 60° field of view, important sections of an object can be brightened or erased, and it is easily interfaced to most computers. Applications include molecular modelling, viewing architectural designs, and showing medical data collected by CAT scanners. There are also limitations. The system is monochrome, images are difficult to rotate and manipulate in real time, and the cost is very much more than most other graphic displays. These problems may be overcome by increased research and falling memory costs.

1.4 PROJECTS

The exercises outlined in this book are not intended to be a methodical course study in any way; rather they are a series of suggestions for further thought and development. To this end many of them have been culled from project titles that have been enthusiastically received by students in the past. It is hoped that some of them will appeal enough to be attempted.

1. Getting colour hard copy from displays is often complex and costly. Try to list the various methods of doing so in terms of cost, performance and likely future development. Think about possible 3-D hard copy.
2. Imagine and then describe an input system where the user can see the screen (or what is happening on it) without looking up from a tablet.

3. Flat panel displays will one day literally change the face of graphics. What are the likeliest types? What advantages might they have over current display technologies?

4. The vector plotter is still an essential part in a computerized environment such as an architectural or engineering office. However, it is still a relatively slow device when several complex drawings are required. What intelligent functions could be incorporated in hardware to improve their performance? Are there any mechanical improvements that might be made (multiple arms, etc.), and if so can you produce a design?

5. The vibrating mirror display produced by Genisco is not the only example of 3-D display systems. Several other methods, including holography and stereoscopic eye-glasses, are being developed. Investigate what is in the pipeline and try to describe the possible work station of 2000 AD.

2

2-D software

The previous chapter covered the devices used to input shapes and display them, but in order to produce a copy of a shape on a graphic device software must be used to convert the X, Y coordinates describing the shape in the real world to the coordinates required by the output display. This process of conversion involves taking the cartesian coordinates which give a shape mathematical existence and mapping them to the device coordinates of any given graphic device.

Figure 2.1 illustrates the basic tasks involved in displaying a shape:

1. Defining a shape as X, Y vectors.
2. Taking the world coordinates defining a shape and mapping them to a graphic display.
3. Clipping the shape to an area on the screen.
4. An algorithm to generate on the device as near an approximation to the world coordinates describing the shape as possible.

The last part of this chapter will look at the standard transformations that are applied to shapes to move, stretch and rotate them, but first the preliminary tasks outlined above will be examined.

2.1 WORLD TO DEVICE TRANSLATION

Most software packages that have been written to perform the conversions necessary to display shapes on different devices have a basic facility to handle world to device coordinate translation. This translation requires two pieces of information — the maximum and minimum coordinates defining a picture, and the actual drawing space of the output device. If the output device is a plotter with a resolution of 0.01 cm then any drawing up to the maximum size of paper the plotter can take can be drawn to an accuracy of 0.01 cm.

In the case of the output device being a raster scan terminal with a resolution of 512 × 512 then some decision must be made on how to translate a line to the screen. A raster scan terminal with the above resolution probably has a display monitor with a diagonal width of about 20 cm, therefore a reasonable initial decision to make would be to equate 1 dot on the screen to 0.5 mm. This would result in a theoretical drawing area of 512 × 0.5 mm or 25.6 cm. Any line up to

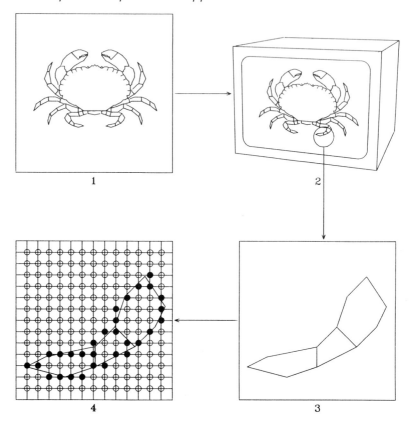

Fig. 2.1 Shape display

this length could then be drawn to an accuracy of 0.05 cm.

In the case of a drawing being larger or much smaller than the actual drawing area of a device then some facility must be given to the user to specify a ratio between the world coordinates of a picture and the drawing area of the device. The method commonly used is to allow the user to supply a scaling factor which is applied to all coordinates passed from the user's coordinate system to the device coordinate system. If the picture were twice as large as the device area the user would set the scaling factor to 0.5: all the coordinates of the picture would then be uniformly multiplied by 0.5, ensuring that the picture would fit inside the available drawing area.

Given that the user can provide the scale to fit an entire picture to a display device, is there anything further that should be offered? The answer is a definite Yes. To have nothing more than the facility to fit all of a picture to the entire display area of a device is far too restrictive. It is important to allow a user a

areas on the screen can be reserved for alphanumerics

entire picture defined
in world *X,Y* coordinates
with window surrounding head

window from world picture
mapped on to viewport on screen

Fig. 2.2 World to viewport

series of selections. These selections are twofold. First, it should be possible to select any smaller part of an entire picture to be displayed. This process is commonly known as specifying a 'window'. Second, the user should be able to fit the 'window' to any subdivision of the display area. This subdivision is normally a rectangle and is called the viewport. Figure 2.2 illustrates this process of selection. The lion on the left is the picture defined in world coordinates, the rectangle surrounding the head is the window. This window is then mapped not to the entire screen on the display device but to a rectangle on it. This rectangle is the viewport and can be specified to be any size, and be anywhere, on the screen. The algorithm for the mapping process between a window and a viewport is termed the 'viewing transformation'. It is an important facility not just because it allows a user to select and display any part of a picture, but because it facilitates the two operations of panning and zooming.

The operations of panning and zooming can be likened to using zoom binoculars. Looking through the binoculars while moving them around a scene is panning. This can be implemented on a graphic display by moving the window over the picture. Zooming-in is simply a matter of increasing or decreasing the size of the window. Both facilities are made possible by the viewing transformation, which works as follows:

A window is defined as (*WX*min, *WX*max, *WY*min, *WY*max)

A viewport is defined as (*VX*min, *VX*max, *VY*min, *VY*max)

A point inside the window is defined in world coordinates (*WX*, *WY*). To

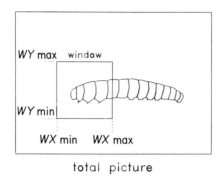
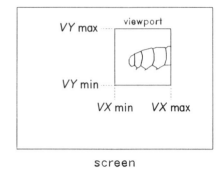

Fig. 2.3 Window to viewport mapping

transform this point to a corresponding point in the screen viewport (*VX*, *WY*) the equations used are:

$$VX = \frac{VXmax - VXmin}{WXmax - WXmin} (WX - WXmin) + VXmin$$

$$VY = \frac{VYmax - VYmin}{WYmax - WYmin} (WY - WYmin) + VYmin$$

This is illustrated in Fig. 2.3.

The following is a specific example of this algorithm.

World coordinates	Device coordinates
WXmin = 2.0	VXmin = 20.0
WXmax = 4.0	VXmax = 50.0
WYmin = 3.0	VYmin = 20.0
WYmax = 5.0	VYmax = 25.0
WX = 2.5	VX = ?
WY = 3.5	VY = ?

$$VX = \frac{50.0 - 20.0}{4.0 - 2.0} (2.5 - 2.0) + 20.0$$

$$VX = \frac{30.0}{2.0} (0.5) + 20.0$$

$$VX = 27.5$$

One point to note is that although the viewport is normally the same shape as the window it need not necessarily be so. The algorithm described will always maintain the proportions of the point to the viewport that the point in the window possesses in relation to the window itself. A more flexible method of

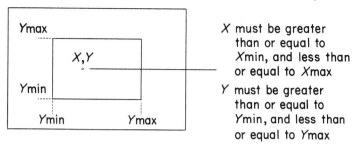

Fig. 2.4 Point clipping

mapping a picture defined in world coordinates on to a graphic display is to create an intermediate stage known as a 'normalization transformation'. This method is used by many of the most popular packages and is described in Chapter 4.

To create a viewport it is necessary to be able to draw lines only up to the edge of the viewport. Any lines from the picture lying outside the viewport must be discarded before being sent to the display device. This requires clipping.

2.2 CLIPPING

Clipping is a fundamental necessity in the controlled display of a graphic image. If it is not implemented and coordinates are sent to a vector refresh or raster scan terminal too large for them to display then any of a number of unwanted events can occur. These include actually damaging the equipment itself, halting the device so that no further drawing is completed, and wrap around where lines seem to appear at random. In the case of pen plotters a further problem is that a negative coordinate sent to the plotter could result in the pen drawing over a previous plot.

To guard against these events and to allow an efficient window to be constructed some clipping algorithm must be implemented. It is advisable to clip the window because this will mean only the contents of the window and not the entire picture need be transformed to the viewport. The various clipping algorithms affect three types of graphic information:

1. Points
2. Lines
3. Polygons

2.2.1 Point clipping

The first of these is very simple. If a point (X, Y) is visible it must satisfy the following conditions (illustrated in Fig. 2.4).

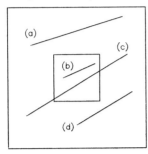

(a) completely invisible

(b) completely visible

(c) partially visible

(d) invisible but requiring more analysis than (a)

Fig. 2.5 Line visibility

X greater than Xmin and less than Xmax

Y greater than Ymin and less than Ymax

Unfortunately very few pictures are composed purely of points or can be conveniently reduced to points. Usually drawings, including text and curves, handled by a computer can be reduced to a number of discrete, small lines. So the facility to clip lines is essential.

2.2.2 Line clipping

When considering a window there are only three possible types of line:

(a) Those that are completely invisible.
(b) Those that are completely visible.
(c) Those that are partially visible.

For an algorithm to be efficient it must be able to determine (a) and (b) very quickly. The third type (c) is trickier, because it really refers to two lines: those that definitely are partially visible, and those that are really invisible but are very difficult for any algorithm to discard immediately as being invisible. Figure 2.5 illustrates these lines.

One representative algorithm of the many that exist for clipping lines is the Cohen–Sutherland method. Its greatest strength is in the rapid recognition of invisible lines. This makes it particularly useful in clipping windows against much larger pictures.

The algorithm begins by assuming that the window lies in the centre of a larger area. This larger area results in nine clear regions for any point to lie in. Each region is given a 4-bit code which uniquely identifies its position in relation to the window. The code is as follows:

1. Point is above the window.
2. Point is below the window.

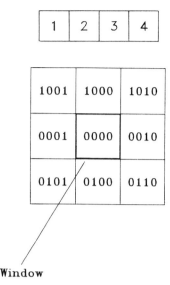

Fig. 2.6 Clipping codes

3. Point is to right of window.
4. Point is to left of window.

If a bit in the code is set to 1 it signifies that the condition attached to that bit is true. Thus if a point is in the top left area its code is 1001. Referring to the code table this would signify that the point is above, and to the left of the window. Figure 2.6 illustrates these regions and their codes.

Any line can be defined by its two endpoints, therefore it can be defined by two of these codes. By a very simple check the algorithm can first determine whether a line is completely visible or invisible. It accomplishes this by testing whether both codes are 0000, in which case the line would be completely inside the window and therefore visible, or whether two corresponding bits are set to 1 in which case the line is completely invisible and can be rejected. To illustrate this last point, if a line has two endpoints with the codes 0101 and 1001 then the fourth bit of each code is true, implying that the endpoints both lie to the left of the window and are consequently invisible. Figure 2.7 demonstrates the cases of completely visible and invisible lines.

If the codes of a line fail these two simple tests then it is assumed that the line is, possibly, partly visible and so they must be submitted to the algorithm for further processing. In the case of this happening the codes are then gone through one bit at a time; if a bit is found to be 1 then the line is clipped against the window edge corresponding to that bit. If, for example, an endpoint of a line had the code 0101 then the line would be clipped against the bottom edge of the

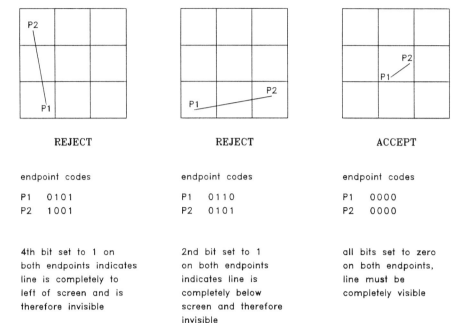

REJECT   REJECT   ACCEPT

endpoint codes   endpoint codes   endpoint codes

P1   0101   P1   0110   P1   0000
P2   1001   P2   0101   P2   0000

4th bit set to 1 on   2nd bit set to 1   all bits set to zero
both endpoints indicates on both endpoints   on both endpoints,
line is completely to   indicates line is   line must be
left of screen and is   completely below   completely visible
therefore invisible   screen and therefore
                          invisible

Fig. 2.7 Simple cases

window because the first non-zero bit in the code is the second bit. After the clipping the codes are re-examined for complete visibility or invisibility. The examination of the bits and the clipping process is continued until all the line is found to be invisible, or until whatever is left of the clipped line is completely visible. Figure 2.8 works through two cases of a line being partially visible, and a line being invisible but requiring further processing.

For any line (P1, P2) the algorithm can be demonstrated by the flowchart (Fig. 2.9).

1. Test P1, P2 for total visibility (both codes 0000).
2. Test P1, P2 for total invisibility (corresponding bits true).
3. If 1 and 2 fail proceed through codes one at a time until a non-zero bit is encountered.
4. Depending on the position of the non-zero bit in the code, perform appropriate clipping action. This clipping action is really determining the X or Y point of intersection at one of the clipping edges. Figure 2.10 clarifies the equation to be performed for each bit code.
5. Resubmit the new code for the clipped line for testing.

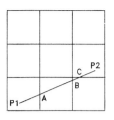

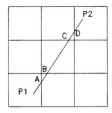

P1   0101
P2   0010

     second bit in P1
     is first non−zero;
     line clipped to
     bottom edge of
     window

P1   0101
P2   1010

     second bit in P1
     is first non−zero;
     line clipped to
     bottom edge of
     window

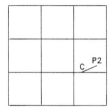

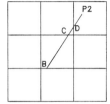

C   0010
P2   0010

     3rd bit in both
     codes is 1, the
     line is invisible

B   0000
P2   1010

     first bit in P2
     is non−zero;
     line clipped to top
     edge of window

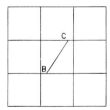

B   0000
C   0000

     all bits now zero
     the line B,C must be
     completely visible

Fig. 2.8 Complex cases

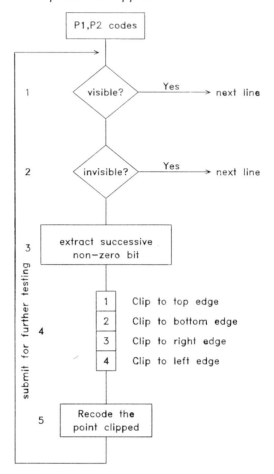

Fig. 2.9 Clipping algorithm

2.2.3 Polygon clipping

If a polygon is a simple line drawing it can be treated like any other sequence of lines and processed by a line clipping algorithm. This could mean presenting it to a display device not as a closed shape, but as a series of possibly unconnected lines. This is perfectly acceptable if the display device is a plotter or vector refresh terminal, but if the display device is a raster scan terminal and the user wishes to shade in the polygon then a line clipping algorithm is insufficient. The polygon must be processed in such a way that the terminal receives one or more correctly clipped and closed polygons. Figure 2.11 shows two typical polygons before and after clipping.

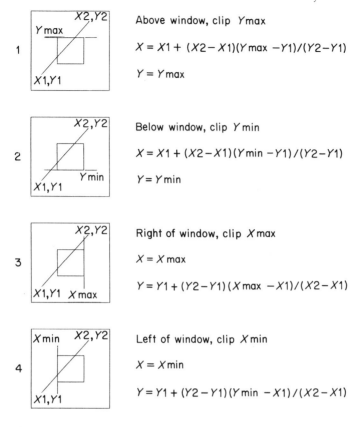

Fig. 2.10 Clipping equations

One algorithm that is used to close polygons after clipping is the Sutherland-Hodgman algorithm. It operates on the single premise that a polygon can be clipped against each boundary of a window separately and any resultant polygons resubmitted to the algorithm for clipping against the next boundary. Figure 2.12 demonstrates this process in action against the right boundary of a window.

The routine handling the clipping maintains an output list of vertices. In case 1 in Fig. 2.12 vertices S and P are both visible and so are passed to the output list. Case 2 is a partially visible line, so the intersection point (I) is calculated (same equations as the Cohen–Sutherland algorithm) and the intersection vertex (I) is added to the output list. In case 3 both vertices are outside the window and no action is taken. Finally in case 4 the intersection point is calculated and, together with the final vertex P which is also visible, is passed to the output list. The output list now contains a definition of a new polygon. The

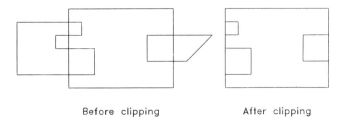

Before clipping   After clipping

Fig. 2.11 Polygon clipping

Window

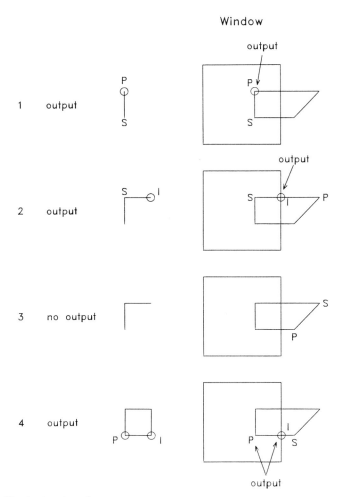

1 output

2 output

3 no output

4 output

output

output

Fig. 2.12 Clipping to a boundary

entire process is repeated for all the window boundaries that are intersected by any resultant polygons.

2.3 LINE DRAWING ALGORITHMS

Any graphic display has a basic restriction when it tries to draw a straight line. This restriction is the resolution of the device. Even a very expensive plotter can only draw a line to within one thousandth of a centimetre and while such a level of accuracy is quite acceptable there are many devices with far less accuracy. These devices present the crucial problem of how to reproduce a line faithfully with only limited accuracy.

A calligraphic display such as a vector refresh terminal requires only two endpoints to draw a line. The line is then drawn to an accuracy equal to the resolution of the device. In this sense, resolution can be thought of as graph paper, the higher the resolution the finer the graph paper. Any endpoint of a line can only be drawn from the nearest intersection of this graph paper. Figure 2.13 shows a line drawn from P1 to P2 where the endpoints are rounded to the nearest grid intersection. This is fine for vector devices but raster scan terminals can only represent a line as a series of points. Viewed from a distance these points must approximate a straight line. The crab claw in Fig. 2.1 illustrates the problem. With a limited number of points it is very difficult to take a picture defined as a series of lines and reproduce all these lines meaningfully as points. What is essential is an algorithm that can take two endpoints of a line and generate all the intermediate points between them. These types of algorithm are known as line generating algorithms. Usually a raster scan terminal will contain a hardware implementation of one of these algorithms. It is very useful to understand the nature of these algorithms, and realize their limitations.

The main criteria of a good line algorithm are that it should be fast, accurate, and easy to implement in hardware. One approach that meets these requirements is to use an incremental technique. This allows calculations to be reduced to a minimum because each successive point representing a line can be calculated with a minimum of computation because each point generated provides the information to generate the next point. Basically one coordinate (e.g. the X coordinate) can be regularly stepped by an increment of one unit while the second coordinate (e.g. the Y coordinate) of the next point can be forecast from the Y coordinate of the current point. Two incremental algorithms that are widely used are the simple incremental algorithm and Bresenham's algorithm.

2.3.1 Simple incremental algorithm

Any incremental algorithm must begin by finding the nearest pixel position to the endpoints of a line and then use these pixel coordinates to define that line.

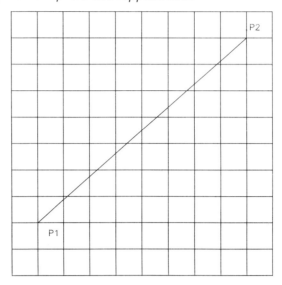

Fig. 2.13 Line rounding

In figure 2.14 a line has been drawn from ($X1$, $Y1$) to ($X2$, $Y2$) where ($X1$, $Y1$) has been rounded to (0, 0) and ($X2$, $Y2$) has been rounded to (20, 12). The next step is to find which is the axis of greatest magnitude. This is easily calculated by making $DX = X2 - X1$ and $DY = Y2 - Y1$. In our example DX is 20 and DY is 12,

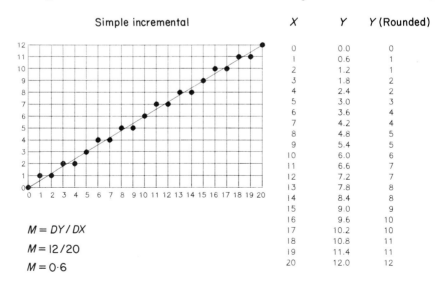

X	Y	Y (Rounded)
0	0.0	0
1	0.6	1
2	1.2	1
3	1.8	2
4	2.4	2
5	3.0	3
6	3.6	4
7	4.2	4
8	4.8	5
9	5.4	5
10	6.0	6
11	6.6	7
12	7.2	7
13	7.8	8
14	8.4	8
15	9.0	9
16	9.6	10
17	10.2	10
18	10.8	11
19	11.4	11
20	12.0	12

$M = DY / DX$

$M = 12 / 20$

$M = 0.6$

Fig. 2.14 Simple incremental

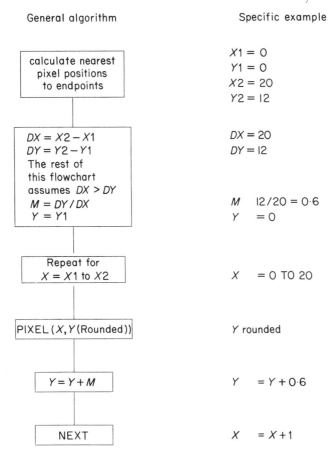

General algorithm

| calculate nearest pixel positions to endpoints |

| DX = X2 − X1
 DY = Y2 − Y1
 The rest of <br> this flowchart <br> assumes DX > DY
 M = DY / DX
 Y = Y1 |

| Repeat for
 X = X1 to X2 |

| PIXEL (X, Y (Rounded)) |

| Y = Y + M |

| NEXT |

Specific example

X1 = 0
Y1 = 0
X2 = 20
Y2 = 12

DX = 20
DY = 12

M   12/20 = 0·6
Y   = 0

X   = 0 TO 20

Y rounded

Y   = Y + 0·6

X   = X + 1

Fig. 2.15 Simple incremental algorithm

therefore the X axis is the axis of greatest magnitude. The next task is to compute the proportion of the smaller axis to the greater. This proportion is termed M. In our example $M = DY/DX$. The simple incremental algorithm then steps through the longer axis incrementing each pixel position by 1 and adding M to the real coordinate of the lesser axis. This coordinate is then rounded to the nearest pixel position. Figure 2.14 shows this process in operation where M is initially calculated as 0.6 (12/20). The flowchart in Fig. 2.15 illustrates the general algorithm together with the specific example.

The main disadvantage of this algorithm is that it is unsuitable for implementation in hardware because of the division logic required to calculate the initial value of M. An algorithm that can be implemented to perform efficiently using integer arithmetic only is Bresenham's algorithm (Fig. 2.16).

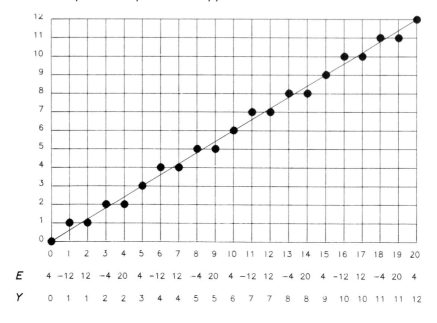

Fig. 2.16 Bresenham algorithm

2.3.2 Bresenham's algorithm

This algorithm gives the same results as the simple incremental algorithm but uses only integer calculations. Instead of adding M (the proportion of the lesser axis to the greater) to each (in our example) Y coordinate and then performing a time-consuming rounding operation, Bresenham's algorithm adopts the same iterative process of incrementing each X coordinate by 1, but maintains an error term E which it uses to decide whether or not to add 1 to the next Y coordinate. This error term E is a record of the distance between the position of the line and the actual pixel generated at any particular point. The flowchart in Fig. 2.17 shows the algorithm in operation and uses two variables (S and T) to illustrate what is actually happening at each iteration. The algorithm only needs to know whether the distance S is greater than T to decide whether the next pixel should be increased by 1 in the lesser axis, or left equal to the current pixel. This is determined by testing whether E is positive or negative.

The example in Fig. 2.16 is identical to that for the simple incremental algorithm and assumes that the line is longest in the X direction. It shows the value of E at each unit step in X and the resulting Y coordinate. The initial value of E uses only a multiplication and nowhere is rounding or division required. This makes the algorithm very suitable for implementation in hardware.

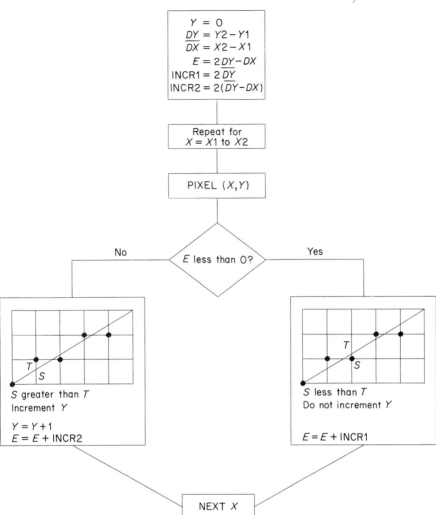

Fig. 2.17 Bresenham algorithm

2.4 TRANSFORMATIONS

The viewing transformation discussed earlier in this chapter allows very little flexibility in the manipulation of pictures before they are output to a graphic device. In order to scale, move or rotate a picture it is normal to apply a matrix operation to the coordinates defining the shape. Matrices are a natural mathematical technique for manipulating shape coordinates. Each of the matrix operations literally transforms a point (X, Y) into a new point $(X1, Y1)$. As any

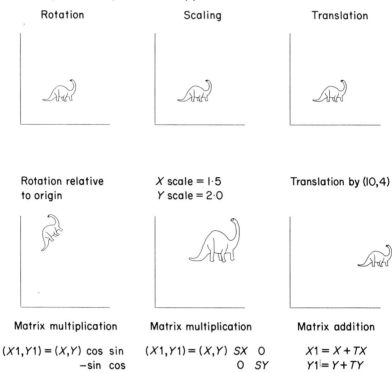

Fig. 2.18 2-D transformations

shape can be considered as a set of points and vectors then an entire shape can be transformed point by point before being displayed. Figure 2.18 shows the basic transformations and their matrix representations.

It can be seen that rotation and scaling are matrix multiplications whereas translation is a matrix addition. It would be preferable if all three operations could be applied as matrix multiplications. This would allow all transformations to be treated in a uniform way. The usual method of accomplishing this is to

$$(X1, Y1, 1) = (X, Y, 1) \begin{bmatrix} a & d & 0 \\ b & e & 0 \\ c & f & 1 \end{bmatrix}$$

c,f control translation

a,b,d,e control rotation

a,e control axial scaling

Fig. 2.19 Standard transformation matrix

extend the shape coordinates into homogeneous coordinates. This involves changing the 2×2 matrix into a 3×3 matrix. The addition of an extra row and column provides a simple tool for treating all transformations in a consistent manner. The third element in the expression $(X1, Y1, 1)$ corresponds to a third plane Z. The use of this element will become clear in Chapter 3. Figure 2.19 shows the standard matrix for 2-D transformations.

This breaks down into the three matrices:

Translation			*Scaling*			*Rotation*		
1	0	0	SX	0	0	cos	sin	0
0	1	0	0	SY	0	−sin	cos	0
TX	TY	1	0	0	1	0	0	1

The facility to scale a point in one or both axes is called axial scaling. Figure 2.18 illustrates a brontosaurus scaled by a factor of 1.5 in the X axis and 2 in the Y axis. The use of homogeneous coordinates to perform this kind of differential scale is straight-forward.

By applying a series of simple matrix operations to a shape quite complex transformations are possible. The brontosaurus in Fig. 2.18 was scaled using non-homogeneous coordinates (2×2 matrix). The result was that all the points were scaled relative to the origin. If we wish to scale a shape about some arbitrary point then we can apply a series of matrices to homogeneous coordinates. Figure 2.21 shows a rectangle scaled by a factor of $(2X, 3Y)$ about its bottom left-hand corner.

The sequence of operations necessary for this particular scaling is:

1. Translate arbitrary point (P1) to origin.
2. Scale.
3. Translate back to P1.

$$(X1, Y1, 1) = (X, Y, 1) \begin{bmatrix} SX & 0 & 0 \\ 0 & SY & 0 \\ 0 & 0 & 1 \end{bmatrix}$$

Where

$SX = 1{\cdot}5$
$SY = 2{\cdot}0$
$(X, Y) = (4, 10)$

$X1 = (SX. X) + (0. Y) + 0$
$X1 = (1{\cdot}5 . 4) + 0 + 0$
$X1 = 6$

$Y1 = (0 . X) + (SY . Y) + 0$
$Y1 = 0 + (2{\cdot}0 . 10) + 0$
$Y1 = 20$

(4, 10) transforms to (6, 20)

Fig. 2.20 Scaling transformation

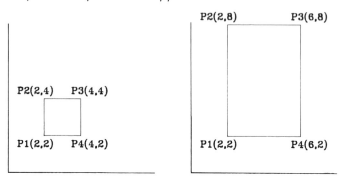

Fig. 2.21 Scaling

Figure 2.22 works through the three transformation matrices necessary to scale the rectangle.

There is no actual need to apply transformations one by one. Complex transformations can be produced by multiplying together the separate matrices to produce one combined (also known as composed or concatenated) matrix. A combined matrix allows much more useful and efficient manipulation of coordinates. The three matrices A, B and C in Fig. 2.22 can be multiplied together to give one matrix:

$$
\begin{array}{ccc}
SX & 0 & 0 \\
0 & SY & 0 \\
TX(1-SX) & TY(1-SY) & 0
\end{array}
$$

In fact we can dispense altogether with the third column. To scale the rectangle we then use:

$$
(X3,\ Y3) = (X,\ Y,\ 1)
\begin{array}{cc}
SX & 0 \\
0 & SY \\
TX\,(1-SX) & TY\,(1-SY)
\end{array}
$$

We can multiply other matrices together to form similar combined matrices.

2.5 PROJECTS

1. Try to implement Bresenham's line drawing algorithm. Are there any possible refinements? How much more efficient is it than the simple incremental method?

2. Write a set of routines to perform the principal transformations. Try to make them as easy to use as possible.

3. The Sutherland—Hodgman polygon clipping algorithm is one method of closing polygons to facilitate polygon shading on raster devices. Write an

	A			B			C	
1	0	0	SX	0	0	1	0	0
0	1	0	0	SY	0	0	1	0
$-TX$	$-TY$	0	0	0	1	TX	TY	1

$TX = 2$ $SX = 2$
$TY = 2$ $SY = 3$

	(X, Y)	Multiply points (X, Y) by matrix **A**

P1 (2,2) $X1 = X*A = 0$
            $Y1 = Y*A = 0$

P2 (2,4) $X1 = X*A = 0$
            $Y1 = Y*A = 1$

P3 (4,4) $X1 = X*A = 2$
            $Y1 = Y*A = 2$

P4 (4,2) $X1 = X*A = 2$
            $Y1 = Y*A = 0$

$(X1, Y1)$ Multiply points $(X1, Y1)$ by matrix **B**

P1 (0,0) $X2 = X1*B = 0$
            $Y2 = Y1*B = 0$

P2 (0,2) $X2 = X1*B = 0$
            $Y2 = Y1*B = 6$

P3 (2,2) $X2 = X1*B = 4$
            $Y2 = Y1*B = 6$

P4 (2,0) $X2 = X1*B = 4$
            $Y2 = Y1*B = 0$

$(X2, Y2)$ Multiply points $(X2, Y2)$ by matrix **C**

P1 (0,0) $X3 = X2*C = 2$
            $Y3 = Y2*C = 2$

P2 (0,6) $X3 = X2*C = 2$
            $Y3 = Y2*C = 8$

P3 (4,6) $X3 = X2*C = 6$
            $Y3 = Y2*C = 8$

P4 (4,0) $X3 = X2*C = 6$
            $Y3 = Y2*C = 2$

Fig. 2.22 Scaling matrices

implementation of this algorithm and include an extension to perform polygon shading on vector plotters.

4. Write the code to accept a line (defined by its two endpoints) and then generate that line as a series of dashes, dots or a mixture of both.

5. Write a program to generate circles and ellipses on either plotters or raster-based v.d.u.s. When writing the code remember that many small computers have v.d.u.s offering resolutions such as 640×250, 390×160, etc. Your program should take this into account and produce a round-looking circle on any display device.

3

3-D software

A primary objective in computer graphics has always been the pursuit of realism. To fox the human eye into believing it is looking at a real object is a particularly rewarding if difficult task. In the 1960s the common method of representing a 3-D object was to display it as a wire-frame outline. This led to the widespread use of cubes, pyramids and boxes to represent anything and everything. Gradually hardware and software developed to provide a range of facilities to help in producing more lifelike pictures. The 1970s particularly saw the arrival of raster devices which really opened up and popularized the use of colour to depict solid objects. In recent years algorithms have emerged to supply shading, reflection and texture to aid in the creation of computer images of photographic clarity. For the production of these extremely realistic images a database must be constructed to contain the information necessary to build a convincing picture. In the case of an object being animated further information will almost inevitably be required.

To begin understanding how a computer can produce such highly complex images it is necessary to begin with those basic transformations introduced in the last chapter — translation, scaling and rotation. By extending the 3×3 matrix into a 4×4 matrix we can not only accomplish those same transformations in 3-D but use the matrix to specify how to project a 3-D object on to a 2-D screen or plotter.

3.1 THE HOMOGENEOUS TRANSFORMATION MATRIX

Extending the 3×3 matrix to 4×4 we have:

$$(X1, Y1, Z1, 1) = (X, Y, Z, 1) \quad \begin{matrix} a_{11} & a_{12} & a_{13} & a_{14} \\ a_{21} & a_{22} & a_{23} & a_{24} \\ a_{31} & a_{32} & a_{33} & a_{34} \\ a_{41} & a_{42} & a_{43} & a_{44} \end{matrix}$$

This would make:

$$X1 = a_{11}X + a_{21}Y + a_{31}Z + a_{41}$$

$$Y1 = a_{12}X + a_{22}Y + a_{32}Z + a_{42}$$

$$Z1 = a_{13}X + a_{23}Y + a_{33}Z + a_{43}$$

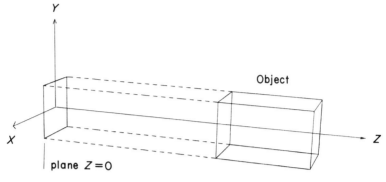

Fig. 3.1 Axonometric projection

The above matrix allows us to not only manipulate 3-D coordinates but to project a transformed object on to a 2-D viewing surface. There are many types of projection: the simplest is the axonometric projection on to the plane $Z = 0$, which becomes the viewing plane. Figure 3.1 shows an object being projected in this manner.

3.2 TRANSFORMATIONS

The axonometric projection is achieved by the following transformation:

$$[X1,Y1,Z1,1] = [X,Y,Z,1] \begin{bmatrix} 1 & 0 & 0 & 0 \\ 0 & 1 & 0 & 0 \\ 0 & 0 & 0 & 0 \\ 0 & 0 & 0 & 1 \end{bmatrix} = [X,Y,0,1]$$

In fact this transformation is equivalent to simply neglecting the Z-coordinate. A more useful projection is the perspective transformation, which gives an illusion of depth. This will be dealt with shortly. First the full transformation matrix will be examined.

The 4×4 transformation matrix can be divided into four distinct submatrices. The submatrices individually control rotation, axial scaling, overall scaling, translation and perspective. Each of these will now be dealt with in turn.

3.2.1 Translation

To translate a point we use the following submatrix:

$$[X,Y,Z,1] \begin{bmatrix} 1 & 0 & 0 & 0 \\ 0 & 1 & 0 & 0 \\ 0 & 0 & 1 & 0 \\ TX & TY & TZ & 1 \end{bmatrix} = [X+TX,\ Y+TY,\ Z+TZ,\ 1]$$

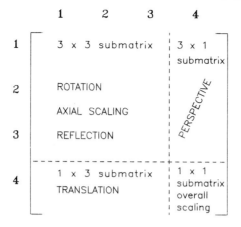

Fig. 3.2 3-D transformation matrix

This matrix translates each point of the object by the amount (TX, TY, TZ).

3.2.2 Overall scaling

The following matrix multiplies all points uniformly by the scaling factor S:

$$[X, Y, Z, 1] \quad \begin{matrix} 1 & 0 & 0 & 0 \\ 0 & 1 & 0 & 0 \\ 0 & 0 & 1 & 0 \\ 0 & 0 & 0 & 1/S \end{matrix} \quad = [X, Y, Z, 1/S] = [SX, SY, SZ, 1]$$

3.2.3 Axial scaling

The matrix controlling axial scaling is:

$$[X, Y, Z, 1] \quad \begin{matrix} SX & 0 & 0 & 0 \\ 0 & SY & 0 & 0 \\ 0 & 0 & SZ & 0 \\ 0 & 0 & 0 & 1 \end{matrix} \quad = [SX^*X, SY^*Y, SZ^*Z, 1]$$

The values SX, SY, SZ independently control scaling on three axes. Figure 3.3 shows:

(a) An unscaled object.
(b) The same object with an overall scaling factor of 2.0.
(c) The same object scaled by 2.5 on the X-axis.
(d) The same object scaled by 1.5 on the Y-axis.
(e) The same object scaled by 3.0 on the Z-axis.

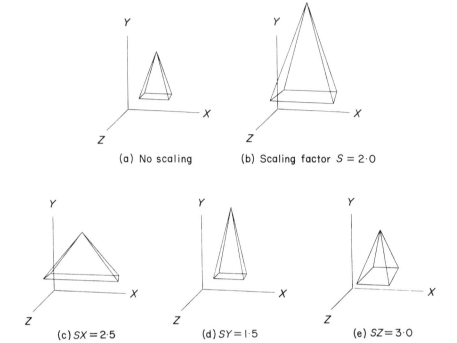

(a) No scaling   (b) Scaling factor $S = 2\cdot0$

(c) $SX = 2\cdot5$ (d) $SY = 1\cdot5$ (e) $SZ = 3\cdot0$

Fig. 3.3 Scaling

3.2.4 Rotation

Rotation is quite straightforward when considered to be about one axis. Figure 3.4 considers the rotation of a point $P(X,Y)$ about the Z-axis. A rotation is said to be positive if it is anticlockwise when viewed from a point on the positive Z-axis. In Fig. 3.4 the angle is a positive rotation.

Initially OP makes an angle ψ with the X-axis, and after rotation, OP1 makes an angle $(\psi+\theta)$ with the X-axis.

This means that we can have:

$$X = r \cos \psi \quad Y = r \sin \psi \quad X1 = r \cos (\psi+\theta) \quad Y1 = \sin (\psi+\theta)$$

so

$$X1 = r (\cos \psi \cos \theta - \sin \psi \sin \theta) = X \cos \theta - Y \sin \theta$$

$$Y1 = r (\sin \psi \cos \theta + \cos \psi \sin \theta) = Y \cos \theta + X \sin \theta = X \sin \theta + Y \cos \theta$$

We can represent the above as a 2×2 matrix:

$$(X1,Y1) = (X,Y) \begin{bmatrix} \cos \theta & \sin \theta \\ -\sin \theta & \cos \theta \end{bmatrix}$$

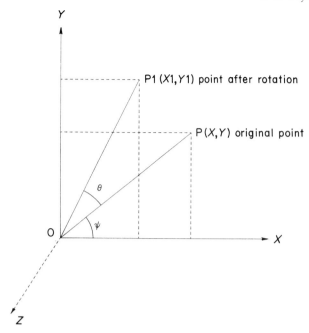

Y

P1 (X1,Y1) point after rotation

P(X,Y) original point

θ

O

ψ

X

Z

Fig. 3.4 3-D rotation

The matrices for rotation about the other two axes are, therefore:

Rotation about y-axis

$$(Z1, X1) = (Z, X) \quad \begin{bmatrix} \cos\theta & \sin\theta \\ -\sin\theta & \cos\theta \end{bmatrix}$$

Rotation about x-axis

$$(Y1, Z1) = (Y, Z) \quad \begin{bmatrix} \cos\theta & \sin\theta \\ -\sin\theta & \cos\theta \end{bmatrix}$$

3.3 VIEWING TRANSFORMATIONS

Several methods are available to specify how an object is to be viewed. All involve the same basic process. A straight line (known as a projector) is drawn from each point defining the object to intersect a plane commonly termed the viewing plane. We have already seen one type of projection, the axonometric projection, which is a projection on to a single plane (in the example in Fig. 3.1 Z was selected as the viewing plane). The matrix to compute the new set of projected points had the effect of simply neglecting the Z-coordinates. This

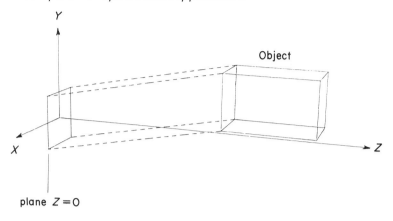

Fig. 3.5 Oblique projection

projection is, however, very limited: at best it can convey only a general impression of a 3-D object. It is one of a set of projections known collectively as 'parallel projections'. Such projections contain only parallel projectors. In the case of axonometric projections parallel lines are equally foreshortened.

Another parallel projection is the oblique projection, in which all the projectors are at an oblique angle to the viewing plane, which is usually chosen to be parallel to the most interesting side of the object being viewed, as it is this side which will be projected without distortion. Figure 3.5 illustrates this projection.

3.4 PERSPECTIVE TRANSFORMATIONS

Parallel projections are very useful when measurements are required of projected objects, for instance by architects and draughtsmen, but they give very little idea of depth. To convey a sense of depth, and depth is probably the most fundamental tool in giving the illusion of reality to the eye, perspective projections are used. Perspective projections are those where all the projectors converge at one single point (known as the viewpoint). Referring to Fig. 3.6 it can be seen that it is now the Z-coordinate (i.e. the depth) of a point on an object which determines its projection on to a viewing plane. In Fig. 3.6 a 2-D picture of the object is obtained by drawing projectors (which can conveniently be thought of as rays of light) from the object to pass through the eye at point E. The perspective projection is then the pattern formed by the intersection of all projectors with the plane Z=0. The projected points on the viewing plane would be connected by lines in the same order that they possessed on the original 3-D object. This takes advantage of the basic property that straight lines on an object project on to straight lines on a viewing plane.

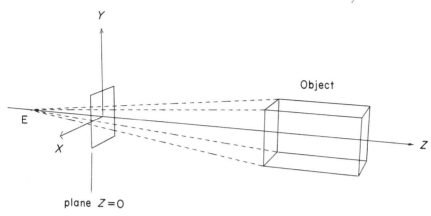

Fig. 3.6 Perspective projection

A simple example to demonstrate the matrix used for perspective transformation is shown in Fig. 3.7. The problem is to derive the projected coordinates ($X1$, $Y1$) of a point P (X, Y, Z). The viewpoint is the point E (0, 0, $-D$) and the viewing plane is the XY plane ($Z = 0$).

The perspective transformation to determine the projected points ($X1$, $Y1$) is worked through in Fig. 3.8. The distance (D) from the viewpoint to the viewing plane is used to control the perspective matrix.

3.4.1 Combining transformations

If we wish to apply a series of transformations to a set of points it is, of course, quite possible to do so by first forming a product matrix Tp by multiplying the transformations together:

$$Tp \quad = \quad T1 \quad * \quad T2 \quad * \quad T3 \quad \ldots \quad Tn$$

The product matrix Tp can then be used to transform the set of points.

3.5 REFLECTION

The 4×4 transformation matrix can also be used to produce reflections through a plane. This is achieved very simply by using the matrix to reverse the sign of all coordinates on one of the three axes. Figure 3.9 shows an object being reflected through all three axes, and the matrices required to accomplish this.

The preceding transformation matrices can be used to project wire-frame objects and perform various operations on them, but outline projection of objects is only a first step in using the computer to represent the real world. Once an object has been defined it is possible to go through several stages

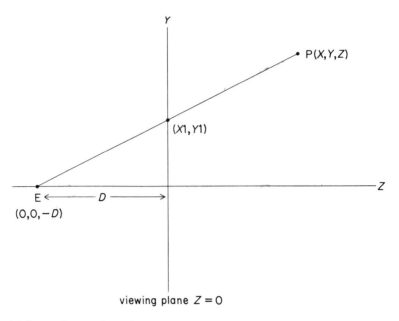

viewing plane $Z = 0$

Fig. 3.7 Perspective transformation

$$(X,Y,Z,1) \begin{bmatrix} 1 & 0 & 0 & 0 \\ 0 & 1 & 0 & 0 \\ 0 & 0 & 0 & \frac{1}{D} \\ 0 & 0 & 0 & 1 \end{bmatrix} \longrightarrow (X,Y,Z,1+\frac{Z}{D})$$

To normalize the coordinates we now divide throughout by $1 + (Z/D)$

$$\begin{bmatrix} \dfrac{X}{1+\frac{Z}{D}} & , & \dfrac{Y}{1+\frac{Z}{D}} & , C , 1 \end{bmatrix} \qquad \text{normalized}$$

$$X1 = \frac{X}{1+\frac{Z}{D}} \qquad Y1 = \frac{Y}{1+\frac{Z}{D}}$$

Fig. 3.8 Perspective transformation

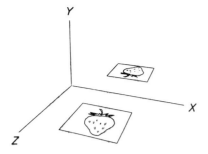

Reflection in *XY* plane

$$
\begin{bmatrix}
1 & 0 & 0 & 0 \\
0 & 1 & 0 & 0 \\
0 & 0 & -1 & 0 \\
0 & 0 & 0 & 1
\end{bmatrix}
$$

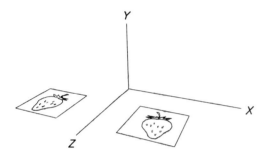

Reflection in *YZ* plane

$$
\begin{bmatrix}
-1 & 0 & 0 & 0 \\
0 & 1 & 0 & 0 \\
0 & 0 & 1 & 0 \\
0 & 0 & 0 & 1
\end{bmatrix}
$$

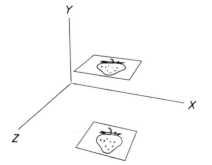

Reflection in *XZ* plane

$$
\begin{bmatrix}
1 & 0 & 0 & 0 \\
0 & -1 & 0 & 0 \\
0 & 0 & 1 & 0 \\
0 & 0 & 0 & 1
\end{bmatrix}
$$

Fig. 3.9 Reflection

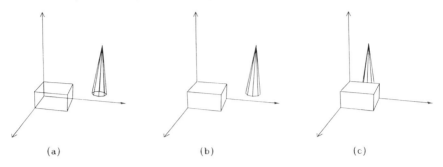

(a)   (b)   (c)

Fig. 3.10 Hidden-line removal

adding increasing layers of realism to it. Figure 3.10 shows a box and cone in three of the earliest stages:

1. The box and cone are displayed with all their outlines visible.
2. The individual objects have had their backfaces removed. In other words they are represented as we would see them if we actually held them in our hand.
3. The box and cone are now in a scene. That part of the cone which would naturally be obscured by the box is removed by the computer.

It is important to remember that 3-D objects can be built up either by measurements taken in the real world or by purely numerical models generated by the computer. In Fig. 3.10 the box and cone fall into this second category. Whether or not we are dealing with such mathematically generated models or objects taken from real measurements we are able to define laws to govern the behaviour of these objects and to attach various properties to them. When simulating the genuine world we must try to produce laws and properties resembling the way in which human receptions actually work. This objective has led to algorithms that remove hidden lines from even extremely complex scenes. This was particularly important in areas such as architecture and engineering. However, to create more believable objects it became desirable to view 3-D objects not as outlines, but as solids. The new wave of raster graphic devices opened up endless possibilities to do just this.

If we use a series of planes (or surfaces) to represent an object then each plane can be given various properties: colour, how it reflects light, how it reacts to heat or pressure, etc. These properties can be used to generate exceptionally realistic images. The process of creating such a photographic image can be broken down into a number of steps. The first is to be able to display a whole series of objects with hidden surfaces removed.

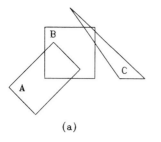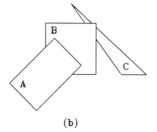

(a)   (b)

Fig. 3.11 Preliminary depth sort

3.6 HIDDEN-SURFACE REMOVAL: NEWELL, NEWELL AND SANCHA ALGORITHM

The removal of hidden surfaces can be accomplished in a similar manner to the approach many painters take to the same problem. The background is painted first, and then figures or objects are painted on top as they get nearer to the onlooker. This method of solving the problem was one of the earliest and most straightforward of the algorithms developed for computer graphics. In effect the Newell, Newell and Sancha algorithm does exactly this: paints a scene which progresses sequentially from the furthest object to the nearest one.

   The main problem involved is in computing the correct sequence in which surfaces are to be drawn. Newell, Newell and Sancha begin by sorting all the surfaces in the complete scene into a list: the furthest one away from the view-point (in terms of the distance between the viewpoint and the surface in the Z-axis) appears at the front of this list, the closest surface appears at the end. This sort is simply a matter of cyling through the coordinates of all surfaces, maintaining a record of the largest (i.e. furthest) Z coordinate on each surface. The sort will produce a roughly correct ordering, but often situations will occur which require much more analyusis before a fully correct ordering of surfaces can be guaranteed. Figure 3.11 shows three polygons (A, B, C) which can be ordered correctly by this initial sort. If they are sorted into the order (C, B, A) and then drawn they will be correctly displayed as in (b). Figure 3.12 shows two situations which will not be resolved by the preliminary sort. In (a) there is a cyclic overlap, in (c) the complication of a penetrating face. Both situations can be dealt with by the algorithm, which breaks the problem down into a series of tests on successive polygons in the list. Assuming the initial list has placed polygon A at the beginning (head) of the list these steps are as follows:

1. Compare the furthest polygon (e.g. A) with the next polygon in the list by applying a depth test on the Z-coordinates. This involves checking whether the largest Z-coordinate in the second polygon is as large or larger than the

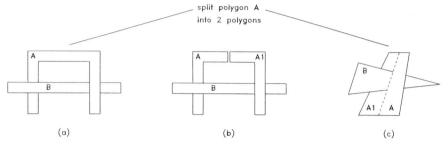

Fig. 3.12 (a) Cyclic overlap; (b) penetrating face

smallest Z-coordinate in polygon A. If this depth overlap test fails then a series of other tests can be applied. If any are true then polygon A is behind the following polygon and so can be drawn and then discarded. The tests are applied in terms of their increasing computational complexity. They are:

2. Apply a minimax test in X and Y. This is done by first projecting the polygons on to the 2-D plane (XY) and performing the following:

$$Xmax \quad (A) \quad smaller \quad than \quad Xmin \quad (B)?$$

$$Ymax \quad (A) \quad smaller \quad than \quad Ymin \quad (B)?$$

If either of these two tests are true then the polygons cannot overlap and so polygon (A) can be drawn.

3. All vertices of A are on the side of B furthest away from the viewer.
4. All vertices of B are on the side of A nearest the viewer.

Tests 3 and 4 can be obtained by testing each vertex of one polygon against the equation of the plane of the other. For example in (3) the equation of the

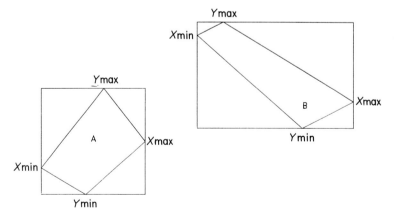

Fig. 3.13 Minimax test in X and Y

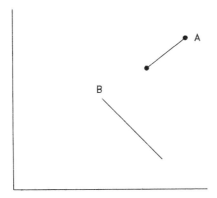

Fig. 3.14 Z-value test

plane B is first computed, and then the *XY* coordinates of each vertex of A is inserted into the equation to return the Z-value of B corresponding to the vertex of A being tested. If all the Z-values of B are smaller (e.g. nearer to the viewpoint) than the corresponding Z-values of A then test (3) is true and polygon A can be drawn. Figure 3.14 illustrates this case.

5. If none of the above succeed then the two polygons are projected on to the *XY* plane and a full test is conducted to decide whether the two polygons overlap in the *XY* plane. This can be determined by finding if there are any points of intersection between the edges of two polygons.

If all these tests fail then the algorithm assumes that A obscures B, so B is moved to the head of the list. When two polygons are interchanged in this manner the polygon moving up the list (e.g. B) is marked as having moved up. The two polygons are then re-examined. It may be that A actually does obscure B in which case one of the five tests will prove true and B will be plotted and discarded. If all tests fail a second time then the polygons are swapped and marked again. When the testing routine detects a polygon marked twice it realizes that it is dealing with a situation similar to those in Fig. 3.12, a cyclic overlap or penetrating face. The routine can now divide the polygon A into two polygons at its intersection with the plane of B. This results in three polygons A, A1 and B. The tests are now re-applied: eventually the polygons in these examples will be sorted into the correct order (A, B, A1).

This algorithm can be used to solve the hidden-surface problem but can be frustrating to watch in action because many polygons will be drawn only to be overdrawn several times. If there happens to be a large polygon in the foreground then a great deal of overdrawing (and, therefore, computation) will be done. The picture of a house in Fig. 3.15 is an example. In (a) the house is drawn with no hidden-surface removal and the fence and other surfaces are all hopelessly drawn together. In (b) the algorithm correctly displays a picture with

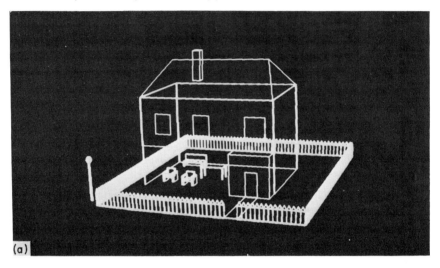

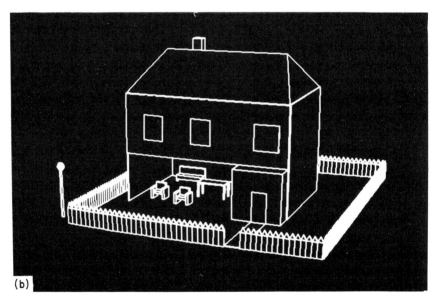

Fig. 3.15 Hidden-surface removal

hidden-surfaces removed but in the process has patiently drawn all the fences at the back of the house only to overdraw a great many of them with the large polygons in the house. The algorithm can be used to draw what is essentially the wire-frame picture in (b) on a raster display by simply filling the interiors of each polygon as it is drawn with pixels set to the background colour. More

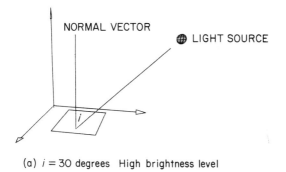

(a) $i = 30$ degrees   High brightness level

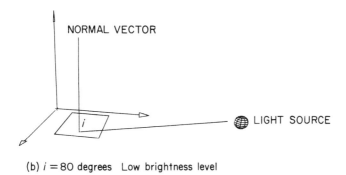

(b) $i = 80$ degrees   Low brightness level

Fig. 3.16 Lambert's cosine law

meaningful in the step towards realism is to shade each polygon as if a light were shining on it.

3.7 SHADING

Perhaps the most appealing feature of raster scan terminals is their ability to display objects as shaded solids. Whether grey scales or colours are used pictures can be constructed that are more lifelike, though not necessarily more descriptive, than wire-frame images.

The simplest technique to approximate real objects is to build them up using planar polygons. These polygons can be passed to an algorithm like Newell, Newell and Sancha and ordered correctly for display. At this stage, when they are about to be drawn, each polygon can be processed to determine the amount of light that it should reflect. Once this amount is known the pixels inside the polygon can be set to an appropriate intensity. The basic method for computing the intensity of light landing on a polygon is given by Lambert's cosine law (illustrated in Fig. 3.16):

$$I = I_s \, K_d \cos (i)$$

where I_s is the intensity of the light source (between 0 and 1), i is the angle between the direction of the light source and the normal vector of the plane of the polygon, I is the resultant level of brightness, and K_d is the reflectance coefficient of the surface.

The principle is that if we have a light source shining on to an object then the intensity of the light reflected outwards by the object changes in relation to the cosine of the angle of incidence of the light. This can be realized more easily by holding a flat object up to a light and tilting it through 90°. As the angle increases between the light source and the object the face of the object will become darker. As the surface of the object comes into direct alignment with the light (i.e. a very small angle of incidence) so the object will reflect more light. The picture of the house used to illustrate hidden-surface removal will provide an example of how such polygon shading can be implemented.

There are two components in analysing how brightly a polygon should be shaded. The first is to compute the normal surface vector. Methods for achieving this vary slightly between algorithms but essentially it is a matter of taking the vector cross product of two sides of a polygon. Appendix 1 lists a typical Pascal routine to perform this calculation. It requires at least three vertices from the polygon being examined.

The second component is a routine into which the resultant normal vector coordinates can be plugged to be processed in accordance with Lambert's cosine law. A Pascal implementation of this is shown in the example in Appendix 1. The routine uses three elements to decide the final brightness of a polygon:

1. The angle of incidence between the surface and the light.
2. The distance between the light source and the polygon.
3. The reflectivity of the polygon. Each polygon should have a tag indicating how reflective it is.

Of course the viewpoint and light source can be in different places, and almost certainly would be in real life. The routine in example 2 will return brightness from any light source.

The actual polygon can now be drawn from any viewpoint specified by the onlooker. The picture of the house in Fig. 3.18 has been drawn with the viewpoint to the right of the house, but with the light source coming from a street-lamp to the left of the house. This approach of specifying only one source of light leads to objects pictured as if illuminated by torch-light. It is more normal practice to add to a scene a degree of ambient light. This is light falling onto a scene equally from all directions. This is more descriptive of natural lighting where objects are illuminated by light reflecting from other objects. This type of light can be included in Lambert's cosine law as follows:

$$I = I_s \, K_d \cos (i) + (I_s * \text{Amb})$$

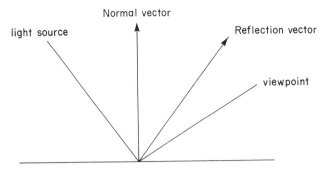

Fig. 3.17 Specular reflection

In the above equation Amb is normally set to a fraction of the reflectance coefficient of the surface (K_d). Its inclusion is important for two reasons. One, it adds to the naturalness of the overall lighting. Two, it ensures some illumination of all surfaces visible from the viewpoint. This is useful when surfaces, though visible, point away from the light source. This ambient light has been included in Fig. 3.18.

The above equation results in a picture conveying only a very bare idea of an object or scene. This may be fine for applications where many views would be necessary before a particular one was chosen for more detailed display, but to

Fig. 3.18 Light illumination

model objects more faithfully several other factors need to be included. The first is additional information about the nature of the surface itself, is it dull or shiny? Many surfaces (such as bottles, metal, glazed pots, etc.) produce very individual highlighting effects. This is a direct result of how well the material reflects light. For example, when you hold a bottle, apple, can or teacup in your hand a very small but bright reflection can be observed in the exact area where the eye is looking. This is because specular reflection is only visible when the angle between the viewpoint and the reflected light is very small. Figure 3.17 illustrates such a situation. A further property of specular reflection is that the highlight takes on the colour of the light rather than simply brightening the surface colour itself. Phong Bui-Tuong produced a straightforward method of including this specular reflection that relies on first mapping surface normals to every pixel before applying the different reflection algorithms. This technique remains in widespread use.

3.8 SHADOWS

Individual objects can be shaded quite reasonably using the simple algorithms outlined. Colours can be simulated by breaking the reflectance coefficient of a polygon into three components: one for red, one for green, one for blue. Each component is inserted into the equations inside the illumination routine and a composite shade returned. However, even with accurate colour tones, when the overall image to be constructed is a scene containing many objects then the eye expects something more — shadows. Shadows help to breathe life into a scene because they depict relationships between objects; their nearness to each other, and relative sizes. They help to resolve visual ambiguities that shaded images alone cannot.

Algorithms for including shadows in scenes are notoriously complex. Of the several described in recent years one, the two-pass approach, lends itself most easily to integration with the Newell, Newell and Sancha hidden-surface algorithm. Though many variations of this approach are possible one basic implementation could be summarized as follows.

The scene is depth sorted into a list of polygons. At the head of the list is the polygon nearest the light source, at the tail the polygon furthest away. The algorithm proceeds through this list, constructing shadow polygons. Those polygons facing the light source are tested to determine whether they are obscured by polygons nearer the light source. If they are they are passed to a file of shadow polygons. In Fig. 3.19 polygon A is calculated to be partially obscured by a preceding object. The part of A lying in shadow (polygon B) is passed to the shadow polygon data file. When the end of the list is reached a file of shadows will have been created. This first pass can be repeated for other light sources. Each time a pass is made for a particular light source the characteristics of that light (e.g. intensity, colour) are also specified. Eventually all the shadows

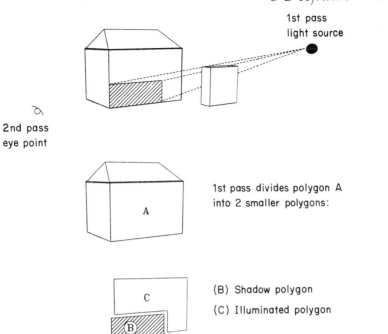

1st pass
light source

2nd pass
eye point

1st pass divides polygon A
into 2 smaller polygons:

A

(B) Shadow polygon

(C) Illuminated polygon

C

Fig. 3.19 Shadow polygons

from one or more light sources are stored in one file which can be referred to when the algorithm continues on to the second pass.

3.9 TEXTURE

The next ingredient in using the computer to produce a realistic still-life is the addition of texture. This is primarily a case of varying the surface colour in accordance with some intensity function (with respect to perspective). The texture of many objects can be generated synthetically by introducing a specific amount of perturbation to the surface normals. The degree of perturbation can be controlled to describe a slightly matted surface through to a highly wrinkled and bumpy one. The garden in Fig. 3.20 for instance has been subdivided into several hundred smaller polygons. By randomly changing the surface normal of each of these smaller polygons a more convincing surface is created. To apply this technique to an object such as a road surface, an orange or a teapot requires very rigorous control of the perturbation. Once texture, colour, shadows and light effects are modelled accurately the final image has something of the appearance of an airbrush picture: it is almost perfect but not quite. The deception of the human eye is just as difficult for a machine as for an artist.

Fig. 3.20 Simple texture by polygon subdivision

One interesting approach to texture is to model the geometry of surfaces using fractals. Fractal is a term coined by Mandelbrot and has come to mean shapes whose behaviour is irregular but predictable. A coastline, for instance, can be generated artificially by allowing chance to guide its growth. The randomness of the evolving shape can be guided by using statistical probability to control the direction and amount of growth. This technique of applying constrained chance to define shapes can be used to simulate many natural shapes. Loren Carpenter has successfully employed fractals to generate highly convincing mountains.

Patterns can be glued onto surfaces by mapping techniques. A pattern may be defined mathematically (or by actually digitizing a picture or photograph) and then overlaid onto the surface polygons in an object. Care must be taken to avoid jagged edges in the final picture by smoothing the edges of the pattern into the surface polygon.

3.10 VIEWING CONDITIONS

Having modelled and illuminated an object or scene as accurately as possible it is desirable to view it with as much control and flexibility as we can. This has led to the implementation of cinematic techniques in the viewing process. The computer can not only perform such things as zoom, pan, soft focus, fade, colour change, streaking, etc; but can move each element in a scene individually along their own paths and at the same time vary the conditions under which a scene is viewed. Lighting conditions can be modified by changing the position, colour and strength of the light source. Atmospheric effects are possible by modifying the colour of each pixel in relation to the distance between the viewpoint and object. By mixing the surface colour of a runway or building into the background colour situations such as fog and mist can be easily simulated. The further the distance from the viewer the greater degree of merging. Given such a varied and elaborate wealth of graphic techniques it is now appropriate to consider the nature of graphic software itself, and the attempts to define international standards to help in the future evolution and dissemination of computer graphics.

3.11 PROJECTS

1. Write a program that will handle shadows cast by one object on to a more distant object. Use the algorithm illustrated in Fig. 3.20.
2. One of the most difficult (and useful) objects to simulate is a tree. How would you go about it?
3. Write a set of routines to simulate various atmospheric effects (mist, fog, snow, etc). Include parameters to vary the intensity of these effects.
4. How easy is it to use the RGB primaries to model a rainbow?
5. Write a program to rotate an object about any axis or about its own centre.
6. Write the code to explode or implode an object defined as a collection of planar faces.

4

Software standards and GKS

4.1 BACKGROUND

Transformations, clipping, line generation, shading and illumination are a few of the vast number of software algorithms available to present-day computer graphics. Where do they all fit? In what sequence should they be performed? Graphic software can all too easily become an intricate jigsaw where no-one knows where the pieces are or quite how they should fit together. To understand attempts to rationalize this situation it is necessary to understand the development of software up to today.

In the early 1960s most hardware manufacturers provided customers with a small package of routines that would draw lines, curves, symbols and text, but only on their own products. A user would access a routine from this software to draw lines, text or perhaps even a graph. The routine called would convert whatever was requested by a user into the hardware codes for a specific device. Such software is typified by the routines provided by Calcomp to control their plotters. The outcome of this was that programmers developed software around these device-dependent routines which would almost inevitably work only on one kind of device (e.g. a plotter) and very probably on only one particular type of computer.

Gradually it was realized that this process made no practical sense. Everyone was writing the same program! So there evolved a more logical and flexible system. Figure 4.1 illustrates this system. A user would write a program that would access one (of perhaps many) specialist libraries to create a picture. This picture would then be fed into a general-purpose set of routines which performed two distinct operations: manipulation of the picture, and the conversion of the final image into specific device codes. Thus the sequence of events depicted in Fig. 4.1 may have been as follows:

1. The user decides to create a picture of West Europe.
2. He inputs some data to a specially written program that generates a particular projection of W. Europe.
3. The resulting geometry (probably a series of lines and curves) is supplied to a general-purpose package which performs two operations:

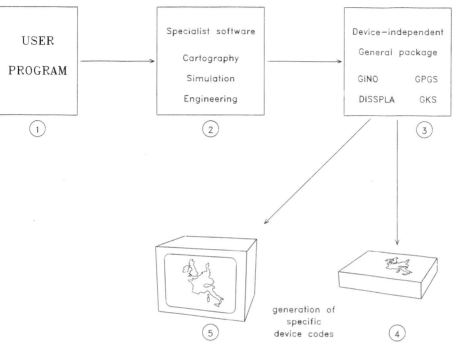

Fig. 4.1 Display software

(a) Scaling and clipping.
   Translation of the picture.
   Generation of dashed lines.
   Addition of text.
   Change of pen colour, etc.
(b) Conversion of the final geometry to specific devices via a series of device
   drivers. A device driver is a piece of software which given an instruction
   (e.g. draw a line from A to B) will generate the appropriate hardware
   code for a particular display device.

A large number of general-purpose packages were written in the late 60s and
throughout the 70s. Notable among the few that survived and became widely
used were DISSPLA in America and GINO-F in Britain. Great care was taken in
the design of these packages so that they were easy to implement on a large
range of computers, and capable of driving a wide range of display devices. To
facilitate portability between different computers such packages were normally
written in standard ANSI Fortran and relied as little as possible on machine-
dependent features.

In parallel special-purpose software often included links into any one of a number of these device-independent packages. Thus a specialist piece of software could call several general-purpose packages each of which could drive a variety of display devices.

There were two problems with general-purpose packages that led to widespread dissatisfaction in the graphics community at large, and an awareness that there must be another step forward. These problems fell into two distinct categories: hardware innovation and software portability. They can be outlined as follows:

1. (a) Input devices, visual displays, and plotters were becoming more and more intelligent, and began to include facilities in hardware (arc generation, text clipping, vector transformation) that were previously the province of the device-independent part of general-purpose packages.
   (b) New facilities were being implemented that many packages were not really designed to handle (e.g. sophisticated display files).
   (c) Most of all, a new wave of devices were rapidly becoming popular which were intrinsically different from the vector devices that had hitherto dominated the graphics scene. These were raster plotters and displays worked by arrays of dots with the ability to mix subtle colours and fill polygons. It was difficult for most general packages to drive these devices efficiently, or to exploit the facilities they offered.
2. The fact that several general packages became popular and extensively used did not help the central problem of program portability. A great deal of software became dependent on the particular general package in use at the installation it was written. This meant that any other installations wishing to use that specific software had to adapt it to work through their own general package. This was costly and time consuming, especially where the general packages differed in their handling of graphic devices.

The above problems with the state of graphic software in the early 70s led to the view that what was clearly needed was one uniform method of providing device-independent facilities, in other words an international standard. The benefits of such a standard were many, but the overriding advantages were broadly identified as:

1. Encourage hardware manufacturers to develop equipment compatible with the methodology and facilities of the standard. Incorporating useful functions in hardware would then help to relieve the host processor and release the standard package to do more useful work.
2. Put an end to programmers implementing the same algorithms time and time again. By embedding an identical system of coordinate handling, transformation, input, etc. into the standard package, the work of application programmers could be greatly simplified. Likewise the introduction of standard device drivers would allow graphic devices to be handled consistently and efficiently.

3. Facilitate portability of graphic programs between different sites and different computers. One standard package would clear the way for special-purpose software to be written with simple 'hooks' into the standard package, easing implementation at any site.

Having realized the benefits and necessity of a standard it was then possible to informally specify the main requirements of one. Such a standard would have to:

1. Be defined by an international group of experts.
2. This definition in turn should lead to a straightforward implementation.
3. Control all devices uniformly.
4. Utilize capabilities of sophisticated and simple devices alike.
5. Facilitate computer independence.
6. Allow picture data to be displayed in different ways on several devices at the same time.
7. Use consistent naming conventions and error handling.
8. Do all the above within a reasonable program size.

Broad agreement of the requirements of a standard did not automatically lead to a definition of the standard itself. In fact the struggle to produce a definition acceptable to the various graphics communities throughout Europe and the United States led to a decade of discussion and heated debate.

By the end of the 1970s there were two distinct contenders for the proposed international standard. One was the Core Graphics System developed under the guidance of the Graphics Standard Planning Committee of the US (GSPC). This system was a comprehensive 3-D specification and several implementations of it have been produced in the United States. The second contender was the Graphical Kernel System (GKS) being developed by the German DIN group. It was this system that was lodged with the International Standards Organization (ISO) in October 1981 as a full Draft Proposal for an international standard. Its main difference from Core lay in the fact that it was a purely 2-D system.

It now seems likely that GKS will gain acceptance as the standard. Core will undoubtedly continue and many manufacturers and software houses will probably provide links between Core and GKS. There are already several manufacturers who are implementing GKS features in their hardware. The rest of this chapter will be devoted to an introduction to the basic facilities and operation of GKS.

4.2 GKS

GKS is intended to be a means of communication between application programs and graphic devices. In this it must behave in a similar manner to a human interpreter, possessing the ability to interpret the requirements of a program, and convert those requirements into the language understood by an input or output device. To enable GKS to carry out this task efficiently it uses the concept of abstraction. This abstraction is the process by which GKS combines the two main requisites of a standard: supplying a comprehensive set of device-independent facilities, and exploiting the full range of capabilities offered by different devices.

Probably the most important abstraction to grasp is that of the work station. A work station is defined in the draft international standard as 'a unit consisting of zero or one display surfaces and zero or more input devices, such as keyboard, tablet and lightpen'. Thus a typical work station could be a simple storage tube terminal, or a sophisticated raster display with several types of input device hooked into it. This leads to two important points. One, GKS is structured so that one application program can use several work stations at the same time. Two, it relieves the application program from having to know anything about the graphic devices it is using. This is achieved by the next level of abstraction, that of input and output primitives.

4.2.1 Output primitives

Output primitives are the basic building blocks GKS uses to construct any graphic picture requested by an application program. In all, there are six such primitives in GKS:

1. *Polyline*: generates a connected sequence of points.
2. *Polymarker*: generates symbols centred at given points.
3. *Fill area*: generates a polygon which may be hollow or filled with a uniform colour, a pattern, or a hatch style.
4. *Cell array*: generates a rectangular array of pixels with individual colours.
5. *Text*: generates a character string at a given position.
6. *General drawing primitives*: access special geometrical capabilities of particular work stations such as arc drawing.

Output primitives can be given up to three types of attribute. These attributes are:

1. Geometric characteristics controlling size and shape. These characteristics are set within the main body of GKS and are, therefore, work-station independent.
2. Non-geometric characteristics controlling the appearance of a primitive (e.g. line-width, colour). These are work-station dependent.
3. *A pick identifier* which is used to identify a primitive, or group of primitives, in a segment, when that segment is picked.

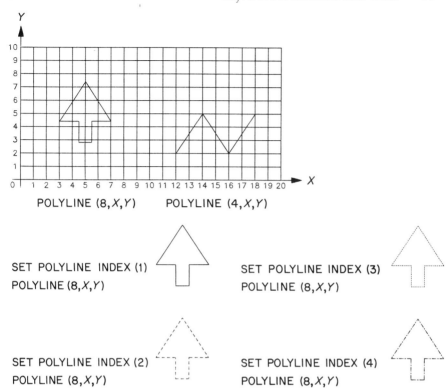

Fig. 4.2 Polylines

(a) Polyline

Line drawing in GKS is accomplished through the output primitive polyline. This primitive can be used to generate one line or a sequence of several thousand connected lines. It takes the form of an array of absolute *X*, *Y* coordinates. It has no geometric attributes but can be controlled using the current polyline index entry. This entry points into a polyline table defined internally in each work-station. The table contains values for linetype, the width of line, and colour. Figure 4.2 shows one particular polyline drawn using all the four GKS-defined linetypes: solid, dashed, dotted, and dashed-dotted. Other linetypes are permissible but are purely implementation dependent.

(b) Polymarker

This primitive is responsible for generating a series of markers. Like polyline it has no geometric attributes but is controlled using a current polymarker index entry. This points to a work-station polymarker table containing values for type

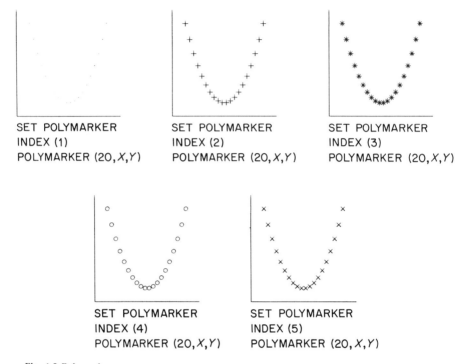

Fig. 4.3 Polymarkers

of marker, colour and scale factor. Fig. 4.3 illustrates the types of marker defined in GKS: dot, plus sign, asterisk, circle and diagonal cross. Like polyline, other marker types can be defined by the implementor.

(c) Fill area

GKS provides the following facility for generating a shape and filling it:

FILL AREA (N, X, Y)

The array of points in X, Y define a closed polygon that is filled in according to the current fill area index. This index is a pointer to the fill area table containing values for the interior style, style index and colour. There are four types of interior style:

1. *Hollow*: just draw the bounding polyline.
2. *Solid*: fill the interior of the polygon in uniform colour.
3. *Hatch*: fill the interior of the polygon using the style index to point to a hatch style in the currently selected fill area bundle table. The hatch pattern is defined in each work station.

SET FILL AREA
INDEX (1)
FILL AREA
(8,*X,Y*)

SET FILL AREA
INDEX (2)
FILL AREA
(8,*X,Y*)

SET FILL AREA
INDEX (3)
FILL AREA
(8,*X,Y*)

SET FILL AREA
INDEX (4)
SET PATTERN
REFERENCE
POINT (1,1)
SET PATTERN SIZE (1)
FILL AREA (8,*X,Y*)

Fig. 4.4 Fill area

4. *Pattern*: fill the interior of the polygon using the style index to point to a particular pattern in the currently selected fill area bundle.

Figure 4.4 shows a polygon filled in using all four interior styles. If a *pattern* style is selected then two geometric attributes must be set. These attributes (*pattern size* and *pattern reference point*) determine the size and starting point of the pattern. By combining various values for these attributes a large range of pattern styles can be selected. These attributes are subject to all geometric transformations. The pattern itself is specified in a pattern table within each work station.

(d) Cell array

A cell array primitive generates a rectangular grid of cells. Each cell is given a colour value in the colour array index. The cell array is defined as follows:

CELL ARRAY (P,Q,N,M,C)

P,Q	Define a rectangle whose bottom left coordinates are P(X,Y), and top right coordinates are Q(X,Y).
N	Number of cells in horizontal (X) direction.
M	Number of cells in vertical (Y) direction.
C	Colour index array assigning colour values to each individual cell.

Figure 4.5 illustrates a cell array of N_*M dimensions. The array of cells is defined in world coordinates and are subject to all geometric transformations. When mapping a transformed array of cells to a raster display each cell may map to one or several pixels.

CELL ARRAY

COLOUR INDEX ARRAY

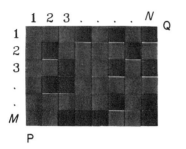

C	1	2	3	4	5	6	7	8
1	3	1	3	2	3	2	1	2
2	1	2	1	1	1	3	2	3
3	3	1	2	1	3	2	1	2
4	1	2	2	3	3	1	3	1
5	3	1	3	1	3	2	3	2
6	3	1	2	2	2	1	1	2

CELL ARRAY (P, Q, N, M, C)

Fig. 4.5 Cell array

(e) Text

A simple but flexible method for defining fonts and a comprehensive set of routines to manipulate those fonts are essential to a standard package. To define a particular font within GKS a series of well-defined guidelines are provided that allow the implementor considerable freedom of font design. Figure 4.6 illustrates the basic rules for font description.

The shape of each character is specified in the implementor's own 2-D coordinate system. The characters must have a character body, a font baseline, a capline and a centreline. The width of a character, including any space on either side of the character, is given by the width of the character body (i.e. the distance between R and L). The font itself can therefore be designed to be monospaced or proportionally spaced. If it is monospaced the character body of all characters is identical. This means that an 'i' would have sufficient space on either side to make it as wide as a 'W'. This gives the appearance of very artificial writing (like most computer printers!) but does allow the length of any string of text to be always known. Proportional spacing requires that a character has a character body in proportion to the character itself, leading to a more professional, and readable, appearance. If the font designer wishes, no space need be left between the character and the character body, and by designing each character so that it uniformly joins the next then joined italic writing is simple to implement. The method of controlling text is shown in Fig. 4.8.

There are four geometric attributes of text which control the appearance of characters on all work stations. They are:

1. *Character height* specifies the height of a capital letter character.

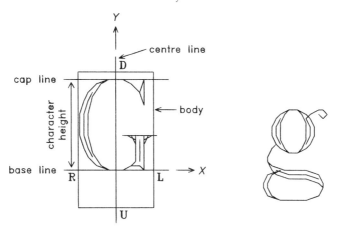

Fig. 4.6 Font description

2. *Text alignment* controls the alignment of a character string in relation to the (X, Y) text position.
3. *Text path* specifies the direction of writing and can be *right, left, up* or *down*.
4. *Character up vector* controls the upwards direction of a character.

These four attributes are work-station-independent and are illustrated in Fig. 4.8.

Each work station has a set of controls over text appearance. These controls are embedded in *text index* which points to the text bundle table in each work station. Work-station-dependent values for text appearance are type of font and precision, character expansion factor, character spacing and text colour. Text font refers to the particular font required by the user. Text precision specifies how accurately a work station can implement the four global geometric attributes. Character expansion factor controls the width-to-height ratio of a character. Character spacing specifies how much additional space is to be inserted between adjacent characters. The value of this is a fraction of the character height and can be negative or positive. If it is negative then characters will overlap each other. Each work station must support at least one font.

The routine to draw text is:

TEXT (X, Y, 'text string')

X, Y starting point of text output

Figure 4.7 shows three different text fonts controlled by various geometric attributes.

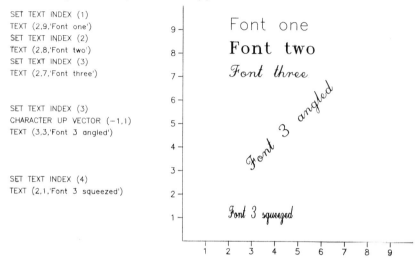

```
SET TEXT INDEX (1)
TEXT (2,9,'Font one')
SET TEXT INDEX (2)
TEXT (2,8,'Font two')
SET TEXT INDEX (3)
TEXT (2,7,'Font three')


SET TEXT INDEX (3)
CHARACTER UP VECTOR (-1,1)
TEXT (3,3,'Font 3 angled')



SET TEXT INDEX (4)
TEXT (2,1,'Font 3 squeezed')
```

Fig. 4.7 Geometric attributes of text

(f) Generalized drawing primitive (GDP)

In order to allow GKS to address any special capabilities of work-station devices a generalized drawing primitive is defined as follows:

$$GDP\ (N,\ X,\ Y,\ ID,\ DR)$$

N	Number of points
X, Y	Coordinates of points
ID	Identifier indicating type of drawing
DR	Data record (containing length, type of data, etc.)

These parameters are interpreted in the work station to produce specific hardware actions. Some of these actions might include:

1. Circular arc: points given are centre, start point and end point. To be connected counter-clockwise.
2. Spline curve: points given are interpolated.
3. Line fit: a straight line is fitted to points given.
4. Ellipse: points given are two focal points, and peripheral point.

In all cases a GDP has no explicit geometric attributes, but the coordinates passed over may first be transformed. The hardware drawing wll be completed in the linestyle and colour set by the current value of one of the polyline, polymarker, text, or fill area indices.

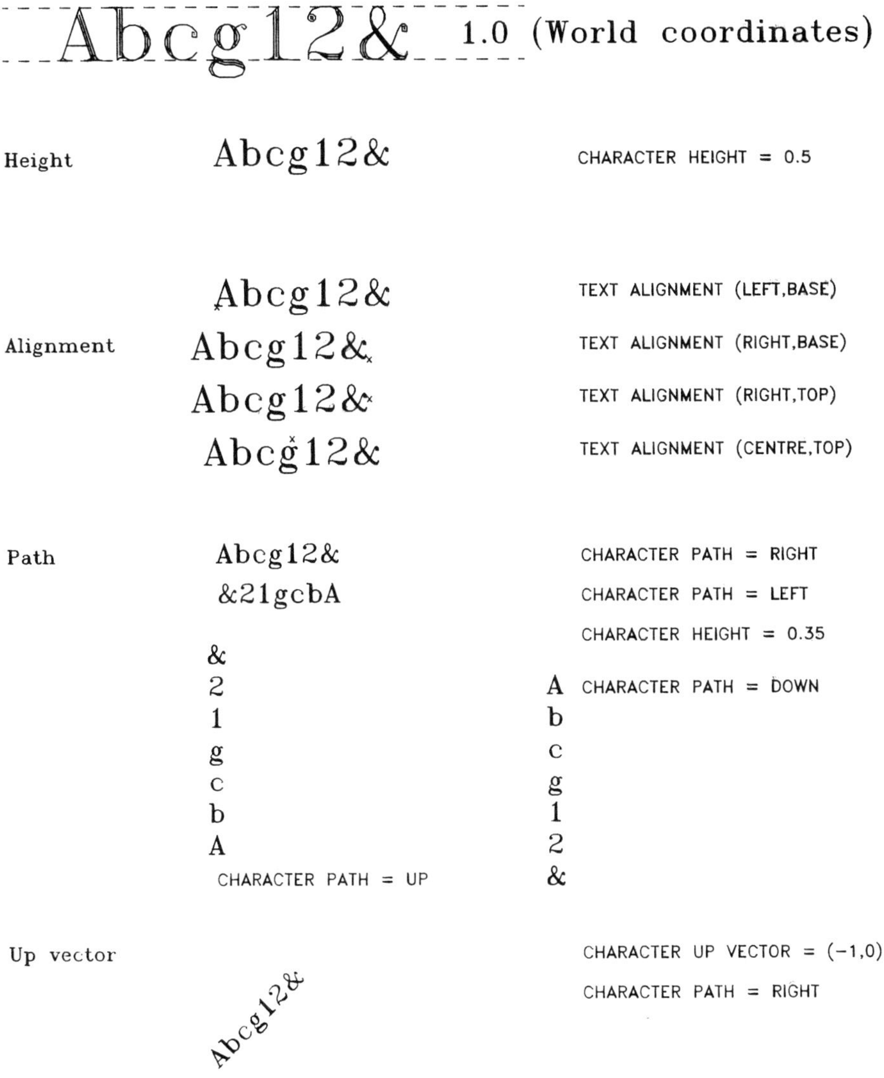

Fig. 4.8 Text attributes

4.2.2 Coordinates and transformations

The first part of Chapter 2 outlined a typical method of displaying a picture on a graphic device by taking a rectangular section of a picture defined in world coordinates (known as a window) and mapping it directly on to a rectangular section of a display device (known as a viewport). This method is very restrictive, particularly if manipulation of several pictures on more than one work

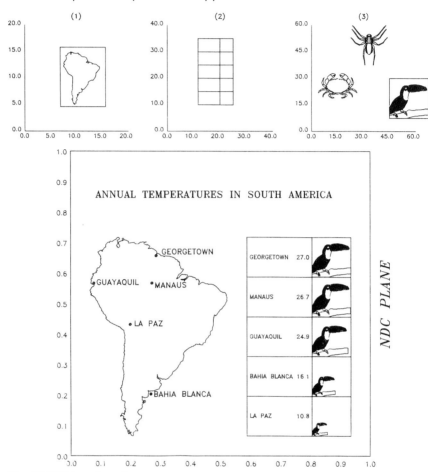

Fig. 4.9 NDC transformations

station is desired. GKS rationalizes this mapping sequence by introducing an intermediate stage known as the normalized device coordinate plane.

The transformation from world coordinates to normalized device coordinates (NDC) is known as the normalization transformation. Figure 4.9 shows three such transformations.

Each normalization transformation entails only two actions by a program, specifying a window on the desired part of a picture in world coordinates and specifying a viewport on the NDC plane. This NDC plane is defined as extended between 0.0 and 1.0 in both directions. Each individual normalization transformation is uniquely identified by an integer transformation number. Thus in Fig. 4.9 the normalization transformations would be specified as follows:

SET WINDOW (1, 6.5, 17.0, 5.0, 16.0)
SET VIEWPORT (1, 0.05, 0.6, 0.05, 0.8)

SET WINDOW (2, 13.0, 27.0, 10.0, 25.0)
SET VIEWPORT (2, 0.6, 0.95, 0.05, 0.7)

SET WINDOW (3, 45.0, 70.0, 5.0, 30.0)
SET VIEWPORT (3, 0.8, 0.95, 0.6, 0.7)

Four more viewports are defined in this example. They decrease the size of the toucan in proportion to the decrease in temperature.

If a program is to make use of several viewports each one can be selected by calling the following with the appropriate transformation number (N).

SELECT NORMALIZATION TRANSFORMATION (N)

Once a normalization transformation is selected it stays in force for any subsequent output until a different viewport is selected.

When a program routes a picture to a work station a second transformation becomes necessary: this is the work-station transformation. This performs a uniform mapping of a window on the NDC plane to a viewport on the workstation device. The calls to define the window and viewport are:

SET WORK-STATION WINDOW (*WS, WXMIN, WXMAX, WYMIN, WYMAX*)

SET WORK-STATION VIEWPORT   (*VS, VXMIN, VXMAX, VYMIN, VYMAX*)

WS is an integer specifying a particular work station. Figure 4.10 is an example of how three pictures defined in world coordinates are transferred to the NDC plane and then directed to various work-station devices. Fill area has been activated to fill in selected parts of the picture. The entire process is an illustration of the work-station principle. The stones can be coloured on a raster display but are hatched when output on a plotter using a variety of hatches to determine which is preferable.

4.2.3 Segments

It is often desirable to split an entire picture into a number of smaller sections. Each section (composed of any amount and mixture of output primitives) can then be individually manipulated by a program. This facility is particularly useful in an interactive environment where a refresh display is an active work station. It would then be very simple to move a segment to a new position, rotate it, scale it, or remove it altogether. Such control is vital in an architectural, engineering, graphic design, or electronic circuit application.

Creation of a segment is accomplished by first opening a segment, specifying any required output primitives, and then closing it. To create a vertical arrow as a segment the following would be sufficient:

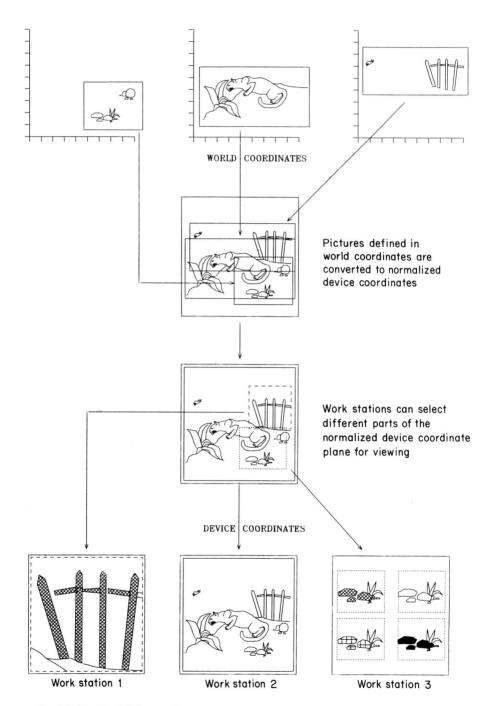

WORLD COORDINATES

Pictures defined in
world coordinates are
converted to normalized
device coordinates

Work stations can select
different parts of the
normalized device coordinate
plane for viewing

DEVICE COORDINATES

Work station 1

Work station 2

Work station 3

Fig. 4.10 World to NDC to work station

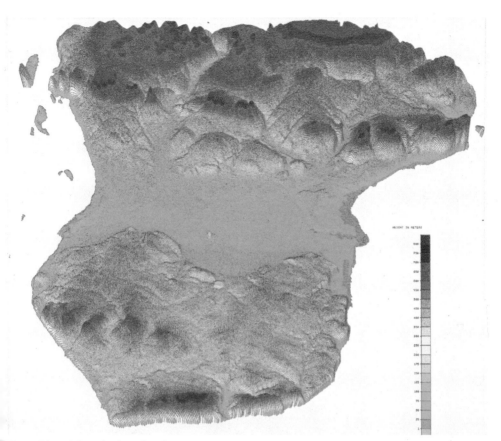

Plate 1 Map of Greenland produced on an Applicon ink-jet plotter (courtesy Applicon Inc.)

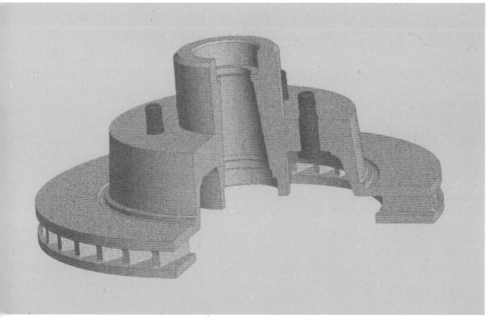

Plate 2 CAD model produced on an Applicon ink-jet plotter (courtesy Applicon Inc.)

Plate 3 Picture of a room produced on a raster display (courtesy ABACUS unit, University of Strathclyde)

Plate 4 Picture of the same room but with different lighting and wallpaper pattern (courtesy ABACUS unit, University of Strathclyde)

Plate 5 CH-46 helicopter flying over mountain terrain (courtesy Rediffusion Simulation)

Plate 6 Ship simulator displaying dusk scene (courtesy Marconi Tepigen)

Plate 7 Ship simulator displaying night scene (courtesy Marconi Tepigen)

Plate 8 Helicopter landing on an offshore oil-rig (courtesy Rediffusion Simulation)

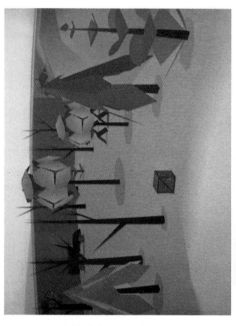

Plate 10 Boeing 757 simulation (courtesy Rediffusion Simulation)

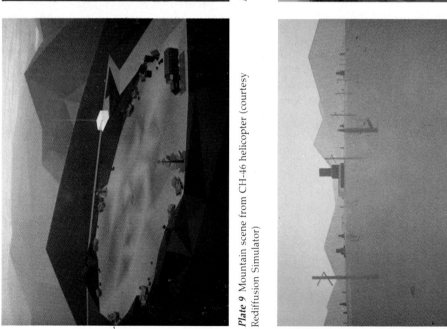

Plate 9 Mountain scene from CH-46 helicopter (courtesy Rediffusion Simulator)

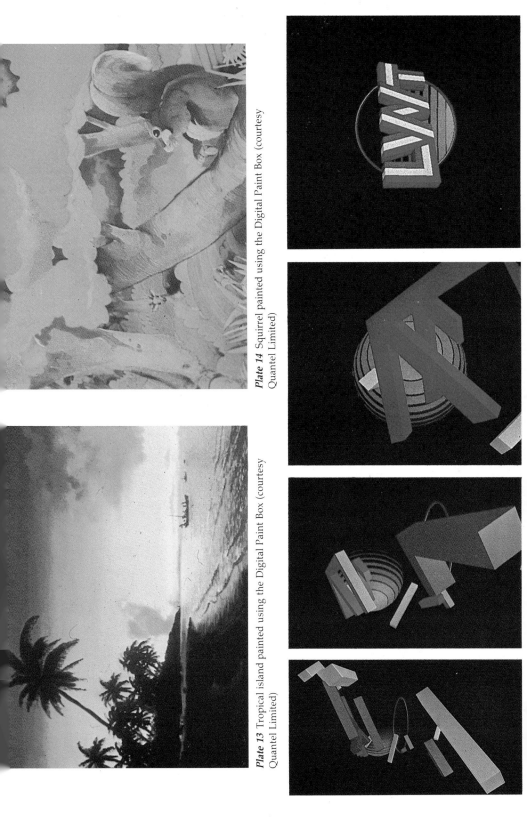

Plate 13 Tropical island painted using the Digital Paint Box (courtesy Quantel Limited)

Plate 14 Squirrel painted using the Digital Paint Box (courtesy Quantel Limited)

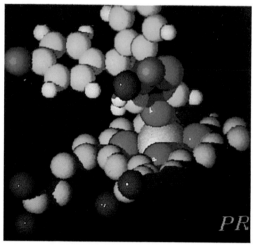

Plate 17 Full shaded model of fungicide (courtesy ICI)

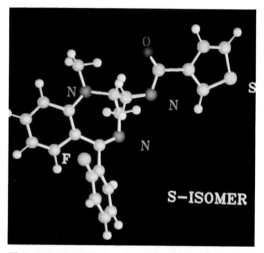

Plate 18 Stick and Ball model of fungicide (courtesy ICI)

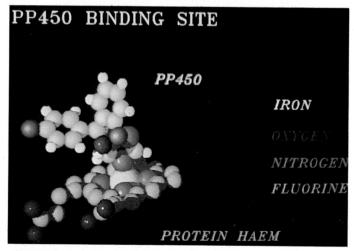

Plate 19 Full shaded model (plus text) of fungicide (courtesy ICI)

Plate 20 Picture generated on an AYDIN 5216 Colour Graphics System (courtesy Aydin Controls UK)

Plate 21 BAR game produced on a raster display (courtesy Judi John)

Plate 22 Fairisle jersey pattern produced on a raster display (courtesy Michael Green)

Plate 23 Fairisle jersey pattern with different colour scheme (courtesy Michael Green)

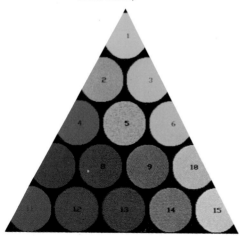

Plate 24 Colour triangle system (courtesy Michael Green)

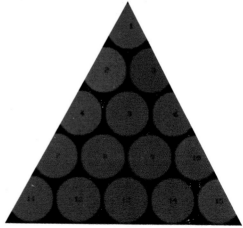

Plate 25 Colour triangle displaying closely related shades (courtesy Michael Green)

CREATE SEGMENT (NSEG)
X SHAFT (1) = 2.0
Y SHAFT (1) = 1.0
X SHAFT (2) = 2.0
Y SHAFT (2) = 4.0
POLYLINE (2, XSHAFT, YSHAFT)
X HEAD (1) = 1.5
Y HEAD (1) = 3.5
X HEAD (2) = 2.0
Y HEAD (2) = 4.0
X HEAD (3) = 2.5
Y HEAD (3) = 3.5
POLYLINE (3, XHEAD, YHEAD)
CLOSE SEGMENT

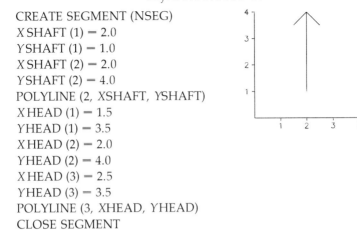

NSEG is a unique, user-specified, segment name.

Once a segment has been created it can be renamed or deleted using the following:

RENAME SEGMENT (OLD NAME, NEW NAME)
DELETE SEGMENT (NAME)

When a user wishes to select an item from a menu, or relocate a picture on a screen, it is useful if the elements of the menu or picture are defined as segments which possess various attributes. These would include making a menu item or picture blink when selected, made invisible, rotated, moved, or scaled. GKS implements these facilities by allowing a program to specify up to five attributes for segments:

1   SET VISIBILITY (NSEG, VISIBLE/INVISIBLE)

This function can make a segment invisible or visible. If it is not used the segment will default to visibility.

2   SET DETECTABILITY (NSEG, UNDETECTABLE/DETECTABLE)

If the segment is made detectable it can be selected by the pick input primitive. This is explained in more detail in Section 4.2.4 on input.

3   SET HIGHLIGHTING (NSEG, HIGHLIGHTED/NORMAL)

If this is invoked then the work station displaying the segment will highlight it in whatever way the implementor decides. Normally this would be either blinking or brightening that particular segment.

4   SET SEGMENT PRIORITY (NSEG, PRIORITY VALUE)

This is a way of specifying the relative importance of segments. If, for example, the priority value of segment 3 is higher than that of segment 5 then segment 3 will be chosen for input or output in preference to segment 5. This is an essential attribute where segments overlap each other. Where segments are being displayed then the segment with the higher priority will always be fully drawn. It depends on the implementor and the hardware capabilities of a display whether the segment with the lower priority is displayed masked or not.

5   SET SEGMENT TRANSFORMATION (NSEG, MATRIX)

All the attribute values and NDC coordinates for a segment are contained in a segment state list. The above routine sets up the values for the transformed matrix in the segment state list. The matrix is of the form:

$$(X1, Y1) = (X, Y, 1) \quad \begin{matrix} A & D \\ B & E \\ C & F \end{matrix}$$

The original coordinates are (X, Y), the transformed coordinates are $(X1, Y1)$. $ABDE$ control rotation and scaling, CF control translation.

The transformation takes place entirely in NDC coordinates. When a transformation is applied the original NDC coordinates (X, Y) remain unchanged, leaving them available for manipulation later. After the (X, Y) coordinates are transformed they are clipped against the viewport on the NDC plane. Finally they are transformed to work-station device coordinates.

4.2.4 Input

Input in GKS is designed to allow efficient use of devices and facilitate sophisticated interactive techniques. To this end it adopts a similar approach to graphic input to that of several other packages (and particularly the Core definition). That approach is to abstract the properties of input devices in order to give application programs an extensive set of controls. The first abstraction is to categorize the logical activities of all input devices into a set of input classes with associated values:

1. *Locator:* this indicates a specific position in world coordinates and provides a normalization transformation number. A digitizing tablet and a joystick are simple examples.
2. *Valuator:* inputs a single value in the form of a real number. Normally this would be a numerical value read from a box of dials.
3. *Choice:* used to indicate a selection from a set of possible choices (e.g. a menu). It is defined in GKS as a non-negative integer; conventionally a zero indicates 'no choice'. Typically a function switch or a set of buttons on a tablet cursor or 'mouse'.
4. *Pick:* used to select a displayed primitive within a segment. It also provides a segment name and a PICK status. Only primitives within a segment can be picked. Typically a light pen or cursor controlled by a joystick.

5. *String:* provides a text string. This is usually entered through a keyboard.
6. *Stroke:* used to input a string of (X, Y) positions. Typically performed through a tablet.

The values from these six input classes (illustrated in Fig. 4.11) allow a large range of activities to be performed interactively. These activities include: defining points to generate lines, circles, and polygons; positioning symbols and pre-defined shapes; entering text and numerical values; using a joystick to define angles of rotation for lines or characters; and pointing to various parts of a picture to perform operations on them. All these facilities require an integrated method of control to direct the flow of input operations. This control is made available by the use of three distinct operating modes. Each mode provides a user with a set of precise responses and actions. To enter one of these modes it is necessary to use:

SET ‹INPUT CLASS› MODE (WSI, ICDN, MODE, ECHO/NOECHO)

WSI   Work-station identifier
ICDN   Input class device number
MODE   REQUEST, SAMPLE, or EVENT
ECHO/NOECHO   Enables echoing

Thus to enter *request* mode for a *locator* class would require:

SET LOCATOR MODE (WSI,ICDN,REQUEST,ECHO/NOECHO)

The operating modes can be summarized as follows:

1. *Request:* causes an attempt to read a logical input value from a specified logical input device. GKS will wait until some input is entered or the operator causes a break action.
2. *Sample:* used where an instant value is required. GKS returns the current logical input value of a specified logical input device.
3. *Event:* GKS maintains one input queue (i.e. a list) containing event reports in the order they were requested. An event report contains the identification of a logical input device and a logical input value from that device.

To define the relationship between physical input devices and logical ones each logical input device can be considered as possessing six properties: measures, triggers, initial value, prompt/echo type, echo area, and a data record. Between them these six properties supply the bridge between logical input and a physical input device. The first two are set up in the work station by the implementor: they are measures, and triggers.

(a) Measures

Measure defines the range of values available to a particular input class. Thus a *locator* measure consists of a position in world coordinates together with the

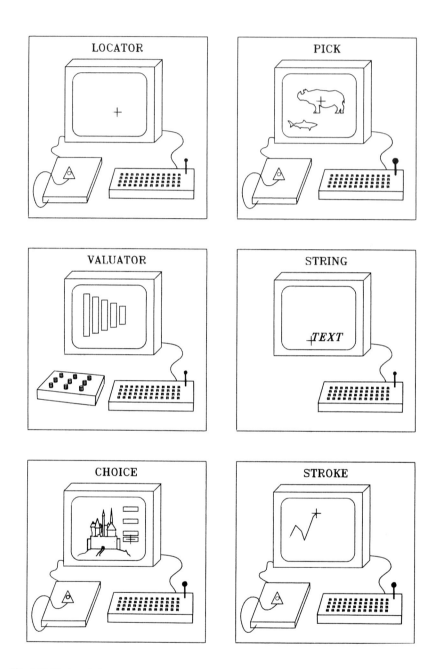

Fig. 4.11 Six input classes

appropriate normalization number.

A *choice* measure is an integer in the range 0 to an implementation defined maximum in any work station.

A *valuator* measure is a real number between a minimum and maxium amount specified in the data record of a work station.

A *string* measure is a character string up to an implementation defined maximum length specified in the work-station data record.

A *pick* measure consists of OK/NOPICK, a segment name, and a pick identifier.

(b) Triggers

A trigger is a physical input device (e.g. a button on a cursor) used to indicate a specific occurrence. When the operator sets one off it is referred to as 'firing' the trigger. This is a signal to one or more logical input devices.

The other four properties of a logical input device can be supplied by the application programmer as parameters to a set of initialization routines. These routines take the general form:

INITIALIZE ‹INPUT CLASS› (parameters)

There is an initialization routine for each input class. The parameters which the application programmer can supply specify the following properties:

(c) Initial value

A value appropriate to that input class. For instance for *locator* this would be a real world coordinate.

(d) Prompt/echo type

Selects a prompting action and an echoing technique. This is implementation dependent. For some LOCATOR prompt/echo types, two positions are required. One position remains fixed, the other is a current position which will vary with the operator's movements. Some PROMPT/echo types for LOCATOR are a crosshair, tracking cross, rectangle, and digital coordinates. Prompt/echo types for CHOICE could be either highlighting the 'picked' primitive or the whole segment.

(e) Echo area

Defines a rectangle in device coordinates. Input devices may use this echo area to display prompts or echos.

(f) Data record

This may contain numerical values and other additional information. For VALUATOR prompt/echo types, the data record must include the lowest and highest permissible values. For STRING prompt/echo types the data record must contain an input buffer size, which is compared against an implementation defined 'maximum input buffer size for string devices'.

Now that the six input classes and their properties have been briefly outlined it is possible to look again at how the three operating modes function.

(i) Request mode

A request function returns the value associated with the specified input class. For instance, REQUEST LOCATOR would return a position in world co-ordinates and the normalization transformation number used in the conversion to world coordinates. REQUEST CHOICE would return an integer choice number. When a request function is issued it has a number of effects:

1. Any current interaction is interrupted.
2. The measure process is started and echoing is performed if it has been enabled.
3. The trigger process is started, GKS waits until the trigger is fired.
4. When the trigger fires, the logical input value is returned.

(ii) Sample mode

This is similar to REQUEST mode. Once a sample mode has been entered by calling SET SAMPLE MODE any interaction is interrupted and the measure process is initiated. A subsequent call to SAMPLE ‹Input class› will return a logical input value with no reference to a trigger.

(iii) Event mode

As in REQUEST MODE, once SET EVENT MODE is invoked any interaction is stopped, the measure process is started, and the trigger is awaited. Once the trigger is fired an event report is generated. The event report contains a device identifier and logical input value pairs.

4.2.5 Work stations

In GKS the most important element in enabling user programs to be truly portable is the concept of the work station. This portability is achieved by two basic features of work stations:

1. Graphic information can be created, transferred between sites, and processed by that site's implementation of GKS to run on its own graphic devices.

2. Application programs can be taken from one site with its own particular configuration of devices, moved to a new site, and run on a second, totally different, configuration of devices. This is possible because work stations will attempt to obey commands whether or not they have the capabilities required by that command. If you were to ask a barman for a brandy that he didn't stock he would not immediately abort himself. He would probably offer you an alternative brandy or perhaps a good whisky. Work stations are very similar to barmen. They will try to do their best for the customer. If, for example, you wish to draw a polyline and request a red pen the work station will either draw a red polyline or, if it is monochrome, might draw the polyline with a thick bright line. How the work station represents unavailable linetypes, colours and similar attributes is primarily up to the implementor.

(a) Accessing one or more work stations

An application program sets GKS into an operational state by calling OPEN GKS. Putting a work station into a state of readiness requires the function:

OPEN WORK STATION (WID, CID, WTYPE)

WID   Work-station identifier

CID   Connection identifier: this opens a channel to allow GKS to talk to that work station

WTYPE   Work-station type

Several work stations can be open at the same time. In this condition they can be considered as being 'ready for action': they are capable of input functions and any segment manipulations (e.g. transformations) will be stored within their segment lists, but they will not receive output primitives or segments for display until they are made active by invoking the function:

ACTIVATE WORK STATION (WID)

WID   Work-station identifier

This function directs any output to the specified (WID) work station. If several work stations are active each will receive output primitives clipped to its own viewport on the NDC plane. Viewports on the NDC plane and work-station windows can be changed dynamically at any time. A set of control functions are also available. These include:

1.   SET DEFERRAL STATE (WID, DEFERRAL MODE, IMPLICIT REGENERATION MODE)

In certain situations it is necessary for GKS to allow work stations to delay graphic actions requested by a program. For instance, when a plotter requires a pen change or new paper. DEFERRAL MODE can take four different values to control the length and type of this delay.

2.   MESSAGE (WID, STRING)

This allows text to be written to a work station.

3.   CLEAR WORK STATION (WID, CONTROL FLAG)

This function clears a display surface. The CONTROL FLAG can be set to check first whether the display area is already empty.

When a program is ready to deactivate a work station or close it altogether the following are required:

DEACTIVATE WORK STATION (WID)
CLOSE WORK STATION (WID)

4.2.6 Transportability of files

To store graphic output for transport to another site, machine or program, GKS provides a special work-station type which can be specified when a work station is opened and activated:

OPEN WORK STATION (GKSM-OUT, FILE, GKSM-OUTPUT)
ACTIVATE WORK STATION (GKSM-OUT)

All output primitives will then be stored in what is effectively a file of GKS controls and data for later use.

(a) Inquiry functions

If a program wishes to find out the characteristics of a work station or the current value of graphic information stored in a work station, it can do so by using an appropriate INQUIRY function. Such functions can return information concerning capabilities of devices, or the value of data stored in a work station. These data can be retrieved as they existed when they were originally passed over by the program or as the value of the data after they have been mapped to the work station.

(b) Error handling

Consistent and efficient error handling is an important facet of any graphics system, particularly in an interactive situation. GKS supports a comprehensive system of error checking, reporting and actions. Each function has a set of specified errors, and whenever any of these are detected an error handling procedure is called with relevant parameters. This procedure will send an error message and the current function identifier to an error file. As soon as an error is detected, all action on the function causing the error ceases and control is passed back to the program. GKS also provides emergency closure facilities when errors threaten to destroy all the work done by a program up to that point. Provision is also made for the implementor to include more specific actions on error detection.

4.2.7 Summary

The prime requirement of a graphics standard is that it should free application software from the vagaries of different devices and different machines. To do this means that the standard should be implementable in any of the main ISO languages, be able to drive the vast majority of current graphic devices, and offer a simple interface to application programs. The principal mechanisms by which GKS achieves these requirements have been briefly outlined in this chapter. Basically they centre on two things: the use of abstraction to define logical input and output which can then be linked to physical devices; and the concept of the work station which relieves the user from unnecessary involvement with the limitations and features of every device.

Whether or not GKS becomes both an international standard and a widely used standard is still uncertain. Hardware manufacturers in America and Europe are offering GKS facilities in hardware and implementations exist already in Fortran, ADA, C, and Pascal. So the future looks bright. Whatever the outcome, GKS is an important step in the right direction.

4.3 PROJECTS

1. What GKS functions would be useful and practical to incorporate as hardware facilities in raster terminals?
2. If you were writing a minimum set of 3-D facilities to incorporate into GKS what would they be?
3. Write the code to provide a solid, hollow, and pattern fill for a polygon using GKS-like attributes.
4. Write a set of routines to manipulate GKS text. Are there any other controls that might be useful?

5

Industrial applications

The final chapters in this book have two main objectives: to introduce the reader to the wide and extremely diversified uses of computer graphics, and also to try to stimulate fresh ways of using this powerful and fascinating medium. This chapter will begin this task by examining some of those areas which can broadly be identified as science and industry.

The first thing to emphasize about application software for graphics is that in most instances it is written by software houses, or institutions such as universities, to be as easy to use as possible. The problems of clipping, line generation, transformation, etc. are kept strictly hidden away. The primary objective is to make data manipulation and picture creation as simple and flexible as possible. Nowhere is this more obvious than in business graphics.

5.1 BUSINESS GRAPHICS

Computer graphics used for business purposes has been in existence for many years in the United States and is now beginning to see some impact in Europe. Basically there are two main areas of usage, the first being to produce material as presentation aids. This includes the use of slides, overhead transparencies, plots and videotapes to illustrate points in conferences, meetings, and training sessions. While conventional methods have been in use for a long time to produce such aids computer graphics systems are taking over more and more of this type of production work.

The second application is in directly helping the process of decision making. This is a more recent but more dynamic area. Where massive amounts of data from a variety of sources need to be quickly brought together for analysis, discussion and decision there is a tremendous advantage in processing it for computer display. This is particularly useful in the situation illustrated in Fig. 5.1. Here data from many departments can be accumulated centrally and made available in a board-room meeting. The advantages of such a system are twofold. First, data from very diverse areas of a firm can be quickly and easily presented for discussion. Second, where the software exists extra information concerning future changes in stocks, financing, supply, demand, labour division, etc. can be fed in to the machine to produce forecasts of the results of such changes. This type of use though not widespread currently is gaining increasing interest.

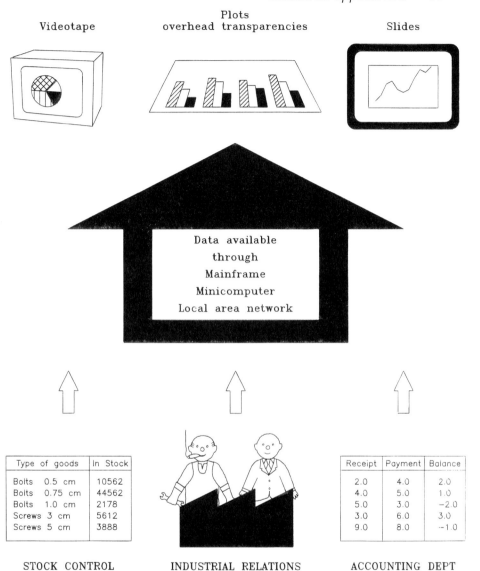

Fig. 5.1 Flow of data

Given the uses outlined it is possible to specify several important requirements of a graphics system for business:

1. *It should be easy to use.* This is usually achieved by providing a menu to aid diagram design and selection. A representative menu is illustrated in Fig. 5.2.

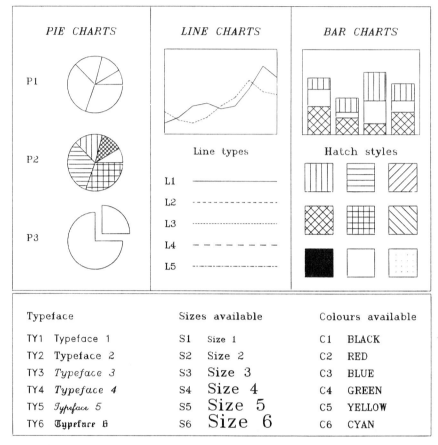

Fig. 5.2 Diagram design menu

Using such a menu the user would only have to point to a particular line or hatch style with a light pen, or possibly type in a simple command. Any chart type he had specified would then be drawn using the styles selected.

2. *Economic.* The system should be able to compete with information displays produced by conventional methods. This would mean making it competitive with in-house designers or an outside bureau.

3. *Simple to update and change data.* This is especially important in an interactive environment where multiple solutions to problems can be tested. It is also important in keeping statistics up to the minute.

4. *Rapid and flexible.* Again, where executives are in a meeting it is vital that the system should be quick to respond to requests for a variety of diagrams.

Determining what kind of computer graphics system is best suited to a particular business organization is often very far from straightforward. Figure 5.1

shows three types of possible configuration for larger organizations. The first two configurations rely on adapting an existing mainframe or minicomputer (which might be handling data processing or monitoring production) to produce graphic analysis. This is desirable because such machines will already be storing the data required to generate business diagrams. In these two situations the software to actually convert data into presentation graphics can be written internally or can be acquired from software houses. Often it is more economic to purchase or rent well-tested software. ISSCO, an American firm, is the world's biggest vendor of such top flight software. Two of its products, DISSPLA and TELL-A-GRAF, are designed to fit on to large computers. The third type of configuration is a local area network of minicomputers or powerful microcomputer systems. Many manufacturers of executive microcomputers advertise that linking their machines together is quite straightforward. This then allows a microcomputer network to be distributed throughout a firm with the great advantage of making the data they handle centrally available. In real life it is usually more difficult to accomplish this networking smoothly and to build a system that performs rapidly enough to be of use.

When a small firm decides to buy a computer to produce its own graphics it is restricted to small popular microcomputers or perhaps an executive machine. These can produce rapid and accurate results but often the resolution is not very good. Further, whereas large firms can afford to buy expensive plotters and camera systems small firms rarely have the money to do so. Two alternatives are possible. One is to buy an inexpensive flat bed plotter and be content to produce fairly low quality plots and transparencies, the second choice is to lease out the hard-copy end of the process. This second alternative is gaining a lot of popularity. It consists of using a microcomputer system (typically something like an APPLE II) to produce a graphic data file (on a tape or floppy disc) which can then be sent to an outside agency. This agency will use a sophisticated camera system (perhaps even a microfilm recorder) to produce a slide or transparency. The process is rather like taking a photograph with your own camera and sending the negative away to a professional laboratory to be developed and printed.

Having acquired equipment of one sort or another business graphics need not be restricted to simple bar charts and line diagrams. There are many ways to display information, and a great deal of research is being conducted into discovering exactly how people most effectively assimilate data from visual pictures. Figure 5.3 shows two types of histogram: both are entertaining and efficient ways of conveying facts and figures. Obviously more versatile software is required to generate this type of output but the large increase in business graphics will invariably bring with it more interesting and flexible methods of displaying data.

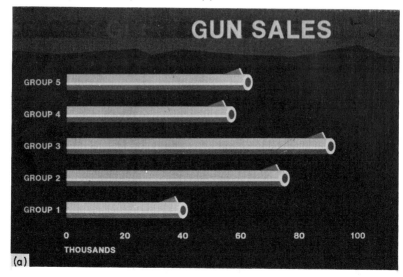

Fig. 5.3 (a) (Courtesy Concept Marketing); (b) (courtesy Judi John)

5.2 ARCHITECTURE

Much of modern architecture centres on the use of clean outlines and form to achieve simplicity, functionality and visual impact in a way unthinkable a century ago. This surge in expression and experiment has had, and still has, many critics. The same arguments sometimes applied to such architecture, that it results in ugly, boring and lifeless blocks of concrete, are often levelled at the modern use of computer graphics in architectural offices. This is missing the point of computer-aided architecture. The computer is there to aid in the speed, accuracy and flexibility of the design and production process. It does not restrict creative design in any way; it is there to help, not to dictate. This usefulness does seem to be gaining wider recognition. A very large number of architectural practices are integrating computers into their operation every year. These office systems can vary greatly in the power they offer.

Perhaps the most difficult decision to make, for a small architectural practice, is what equipment to buy for their entry into computer-aided design. Frequently the money is not available for a full production system so it is often necessary to begin with a small, normally CP/M based microcomputer. Together with simple software and an inexpensive flat-bed plotter such micro-systems can be bought very cheaply. At this level they are probably more useful as an introduction to computers in the office. Although they can offer word processing, perform area calculations and perspective projections, even generate costing graphs, they are too limited in the data they can process, the computations they can perform, or the sophistication of output, to be of value in the actual production process. To go to a system capable of being genuinely useful requires at least a minicomputer with disc storage, several terminals, a good quality large plotter and very good software. A system of this type would probably contain at least one vector refresh high resolution display with some hardware facility for rotation, zooming and perhaps clipping. The final stage is a complete design and production system for larger practices. These are extremely expensive but highly adaptable. A typical configuration might be:

1. A powerful minicomputer.
2. Extensive disc storage.
3. Multiple terminals.
4. Large drum or flat-bed plotter.
5. High resolution vector refresh display.
6. High resolution raster display.
7. Electrostatic or sophisticated ink-jet plotter.
8. Large digitizer.

When some equipment has been purchased, what will it be used for? Broadly speaking there are three main areas where computers are useful: traditional 2-D drafting; 3-D modelling; and performance analysis.

5.2.1 2-D drafting

The workhorse of virtually any architectural office is the production of accurate design plans. These are produced in great quantity, and can range from the simple dimensions of a room, to an integrated set of overlays showing furniture, lighting and heating arrangements throughout an entire office block or hotel. Using a computer system to automate the process of producing these is the most widely known use of computer graphics in architecture. In a typical office environment a designer would use a large digitizing board to help input architectural data. Once the data is inside the machine he can manipulate sections of the drawing very easily. To facilitate the designer in this process most software allows any segment of the picture to be rotated, scaled, copied, moved, deleted, or filled in. Quite often software also allows the architect to zoom in on a small part of the drawing to make very small adjustments. The major disadvantage in such a system is inputting the design in the first place. This can take a long time even with the help of a selection of menu aids. Once the design is defined the computer does then make changing elements of the design very easy. Figure 5.4 is a diagram produced by the General Drafting System (Applied Research, Cambridge) illustrating the flexibility of architectural software.

5.2.2 3-D modelling

Creating a 3-D image of a design is one of the most exciting applications of computer graphics. It is relatively easy to take X, Y, Z data and create a wire-frame perspective drawing from any viewpoint. This can be very useful in creating a model of a building, putting this model in an existing or envisaged environment, and assessing its visual impact. Taking this visualization further a lot of software has become recently available to allow 3-D building models to be shaded in. This has opened a door to a set of possibilities yet to be fully explored. It allows architects to create multiple views of a building each of which shows its appearance at different times of the day. Some architectural contracts also include the interior design of a building. This is an area where shaded graphics can be immensely helpful. A designer can create several views of a room showing a variety of seating arrangements, windows, doors, wall colours and lighting systems. The customer can then select, or specify, whatever design appeals most. These coloured models can be built up by using the software discussed in Chapter 4. Plates 3 and 4 show two views of a room interior produced by a commercial architetural package.

5.2.3 Performance analysis

Decisions about the performance of a proposed building in the real world are very complex. Specialist software is marketed which helps designers assess specific problems. These problems include:

1. How best to utilize space (e.g. placing bookshelves, tables and chairs in a library).
2. Where to position essential equipment in hospitals and factories.
3. How buildings react to annual variations in humidity and temperature.
4. Where to lay wires, pipes and meters for easy access.
5. How different types of windows, glazing, shutters, doors affect room temperatures, especially in winter and summer.
6. Cost analysis of materials.

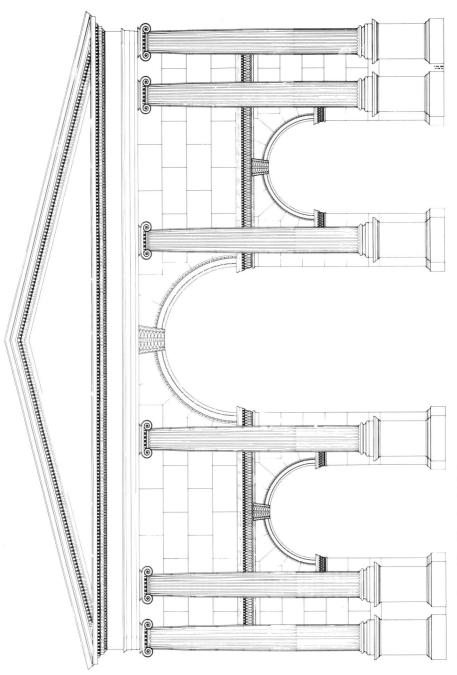

Fig. 5.4 (Courtesy General Drafting Cambridge)

All these can be analysed by the computer and graphs, charts and data tables returned.

The preceding three uses provide several substantial advantages: fast, accurate drawings; flexible models; extensive analysis and simulation; overall coordination from one central data-base; and a continuous cost analysis. There also remain several stumbling blocks. First, all the equipment and programs can cost a great deal of money, but, more fundamentally, there is still a widespread dislike of computers amongst many architects. This is very difficult to overcome, especially when designers are told that they will have to undergo quite lengthy training to operate a fully computerized system. It is almost impossible to combine hardware and software to overcome buzz-words and technical concepts to allow designers to understand and easily use drafting and modelling systems.

There are many possible forecasts for the future of computer graphics in architecture, some of them just around the corner, others slightly further away. One obvious area for growth is 3-D modelling. It will slowly become more and more accepted to create a shaded image of a building in its proposed environment and simulate movement around it and inside it. This might well lead to offices preparing video tapes for clients of just such an animated view of their designs. In line with this it is probable that expert systems will emerge which enable the architect to tell the system exactly what he wants it to do and how it will let him do it. This has been a drawback for too long; architectural practices have always had to adapt themselves to a system instead of the other way around. These two advances will, it is hoped, lead to the situation where an architect can use a computerized system to design a building precisely how he wants to and then show an equally precise visualization to his client.

5.3 COMPUTER IMAGE GENERATION

In the modern world of high technology there are many areas where training or simulation are prohibitively expensive. To train pilots for civil and military aircraft, for ships, submarines and space missions, requires large resources of time, money and equipment. To model products or processes in engineering, power station control, computer-aided design, chemistry, oil-drilling, or medicine, demands equally expensive resources. One branch of computer graphics that can help in a very dynamic way in these areas is computer image generation. This involves simulating part of the real world and giving interactive control of that simulation to an operator. This might be a biologist rotating a string of molecules or a surgeon analysing cancer growth. This section intends to look at one large slice of image generation, real-time simulation systems for aircraft and ships. Simulations of this type constitute what are undoubtedly the greatest video games of all, but with very concrete benefits in savings and safety.

5.3.1 Ship simulators

A pilot and navigator can use a ship simulator to sail through known and unknown waters, and test their ability to react to a series of situations. The actual view through the bridge window will change in perfect accordance to their management of bridge controls, to external weather conditions and even to the movement of other ships. They can sail from night-time through to dawn and observe buoys, harbours and other ships gradually appearing through the early morning haze, or they can sail from dusk into night and watch the twinkling lights of other vessels and towns becoming brighter. In all situations they will behave exactly as if they were at sea. The benefits of such a realistic simulation were summarized in 1976 by Marconi Radar (a leading maker of ship simulators).

1. To exercise deck officers, promoting greater safety.
2. Initial training in pilotage.
3. Exercises in handling dangerous situations (loss of propulsion, loss of communications, onset of fog, etc.).
4. Studying the handling of unfamiliar ships.
5. Familarization with special effects such as shallow water or interaction at closer quarters.
6. Research, for ship design and as an aid to the elaboration of safe traffic rules.
7. Planning of ports and approaches.

Taking Marconi Radar systems as an example the following features were implemented in their simulators to provide the previous benefits:

1. Visual systems to cover all-weather operations, by day or night.
2. An adequate number of other ships to be shown, some at least under control during an exercise so that their courses and speeds can be changed.
3. Large numbers of lights to be simulated, to cover the cases of fishing fleets, approaches in populated areas, etc.
4. 'Realism' in the scene to be sufficient to give the trainee involvement in the exercise and to provide the visual cues he relies on.

The ship simulators produced by Marconi are known under the general heading TEPIGEN (Television Picture Generator). The operation of the computer system is shown in Fig. 5.5.

In the above system all the performance characteristics of the ship being simulated must be measured and modelled mathematically in a simulation computer. This model responds to the use of controls in a mock-up bridge and the ship proceeds accordingly. The position and heading of the ship are fed continuously from the simulation computer to the scenario computer, which contains a mathematical model of all scenery within viewing distance. The scenario computer also updates the heading and position of 'other ships' within the

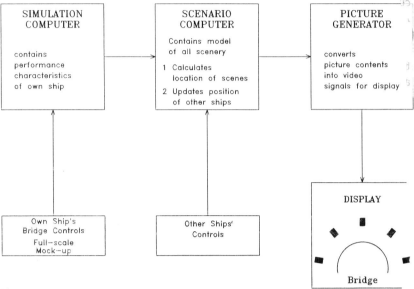

Fig. 5.5 Tepigen computer system

scene. These other ships can be pre-programmed, or can be controlled by external instructor. An entire picture can now be fed to the Picture Genei which translates the picture into video signals suitable for t.v. projection. entire process occurs about 25 times a second to provide 'real-time' animat In Fig. 5.5 the video signals are channelled to five projectors which project images on to the rear of a curved viewing screen. This viewing screen is in fi of the mock-up bridge, making it independent of the projectors. The fiek view seen from the bridge is 40° for each projector. In this example field of v would be 200°.

Plates 6 and 7 show a daylight and night-time scene from a TEPIGEN si lator. The scenes inside the scenario computer are held as a number of m each defined as a series of planar faces. When pulled into the field of view faces are rapidly processed so that only those visible to the viewer are passe the picture generator. Typical elements of a scene can consist not only of isla and other ships but also of harbours, mountains, buoys, landmarks, bow w and wash of other ships, clusters of lights, and even stars. All combine togetl to make a simulation as real, vivid and useful as possible.

5.3.2 Flight simulators

The remainder of this section will look at the current state of civil and military aircraft simulators in general, followed by detailed examinations of two in parti ilar. The first of these simulators is the CT-5, a very advanced Anglo–American system, the second is a description of a helmet mounted projector for flight simulation.

The most well-known use of real-time simulators is in the field of aviation raining for pilots. Computer-controlled flight simulators emerged in the 1960s and have developed over the years, until today they are capable of generating extremely realistic imagery and simulating an extensive range of aircraft and situations. Their usefulness lies in three key areas:

1. They can provide training in a wide range of situations and utilize the experience of instructors. In a typical simulation an instructor can take a new pilot through bad weather conditions, complicated landings, engine failures and emergency procedures. These are very difficult areas in which to gain experience in actual training flights.

2. Emergency landings, air or ground collisions, fire, control malfunctions and storm weather can all be learned without physical danger to a flight crew. This is important both in simulating existing aircraft and in testing new, experimental prototypes. In military exercises, where combat situations need to be simulated as realistically as possible, the safety of a simulator is essential.

The cost of training pilots in all these situations is extremely high if carried out in actual training flights. The cost of using a simulator breaks down into two parts but remains substantially cheaper. The first is the capital outlay required in either developing a system from scratch, or buying an existing system. To develop a new simulator requires generating a complete mathematical model of an aircraft and producing software to imitate its proposed operating environment. The physical controls must then be duplicated and linked into the computer simulator. This development stage can take more than two years. However, once a simulator is actually installed then its running costs become only a small fraction (approximately 10%) of the equivalent training hours in a real aircraft.

Simulators can be built to imitate virtually any conceivable type of aircraft, to re-create flight paths, airports, oil-rigs at sea, or any other possible environment. In practice simulators are normally designed for large commercial planes, a few helicopters, and most military aircraft. The majority of these simulators possess similar characteristics. They require re-creating the control cabin down to the smallest instrument and, once seated at the controls, the pilot or navigator can look out of the windows directly in front of them and expect to see the same scenery as if they were actually airborne. In fact behind the windows are high-quality displays upon which the computer generates imagery. Sophisticated simulators also contain some form of motion-cue. This comes from mechanical apparatus beneath the control cabin which tilts the cabin in relation to wind-speed and the angle of flying.

Fig. 5.6 (a)(Courtesy Marconi Radar); (b) (Courtesy Marconi Radar)

The computer images fed to a display vary greatly between different systems. The most important criteria in determining the 'realism' of the images are the amount of polygons which can be processed and displayed to form a continuously moving image and the type of display chosen to display the image. Simply, the more polygons (or surfaces) which can be generated, the more detail and texture can be included in the final image. A typical system might display about 500 polygons in a day-time simulation. These polygons would be taken from a much larger data-base. As aircraft get nearer to a particular terrain feature (perhaps a hangar or runway) then the level of detail will increase in proportion. In Fig. 5.6 two pictures from a helicopter simulator (produced by Marconi Radar) illustrate a helicopter landing near a bridge. The view above shows the amount of detail necessary when the helicopter is flying reasonably fast several hundred feet up. At this height the detail can be fairly general. To heighten the effectiveness of the image textures can be added to polygons to represent different types of terrain feature (e.g. trees, water, fields, etc.). The second picture shows the same helicopter landing near the bridge. The database can now generate more information and detail, resulting in individual bricks appearing on the bridge and in textured railway tracks.

Standards for flight simulators are laid down by various international regulatory authorities. Chief among these is the Federal Aviation Authority. Phase 2 and 3 of their Advanced Simulation Plan outline very stringent visual requirements for airline simulators. To transfer training time from aircraft to simulator these requirements must be met. Some of the performance standards laid down by the FAA are:

Phase 2   The simulator should accurately model out-of-the window scenes of real-world airports. A large variety of airfield and topographical features should be available under an extremely wide range of weather conditions. The simulator should be able to simulate a mid-air collision with another aircraft or airport service truck.

Phase 3   This phase is intended to specify a simulator which can handle all normal flight crew training and checking. This includes initial and advanced training. It requires that a crew perform integrated training in a daylight cockpit environment with bright, high quality scenes representing many types of abnormal weather conditions. Besides this the simulator should be able to show features known to cause landing illusions; these include short runways, landing over water, runway gradient and rising terrain.

The accepted world leaders in advanced simulation systems are Rediffusion Simulation. Together with Evans and Sutherland Computer Corporation they have developed the NOVOVIEW SP3T system which is the first simulator to meet all the requirements of Phase 3. This system needed very advanced interactive graphics to produce fast, high-quality visual images. Figure 5.7 shows a

Fig. 5.7 Approach to a frigate (Courtesy Rediffusion Simulation)

scene generated from a NOVOVIEW SP3T of an approach to a frigate. The detail and texture effects are of a very high standard. NOVOVIEW SP3T can also add 2-D texture to enhance picture quality. Textured effects are produced by overlaying several basic patterns of varying size to give different texture arrangements. Small pattern detail gives speed and height cues when an aircraft is close to the ground. Larger texture patterns applied to extensive surfaces such as terrain or clouds contribute towards an overall impression.

Additionally, the texture may be made dynamic to simulate blowing sand, snow or smoke. Plate 8 shows a helicopter operating onto an offshore oil rig. Here the texture patterning has been applied to sea and sky.

The first simulator visual systems, which appeared during the 1960s, relied on a camera 'flying' over a model to provide pictures on a screen in front of the flight deck window. The technique lacked flexibility of modelling and field of view so it was replaced in the 1970s by computer-generated images. In the simulation systems described up to this point these computer images were displayed through individual monitors (usually high quality shadow-mask CRTs) mounted around the flight deck windows. Each module was optically arranged for the viewpoint of a single observer, making it difficult for a crew member to look to a different window and see an intelligible picture from his viewpoint. A recent development by Rediffusion Simulation in the way in

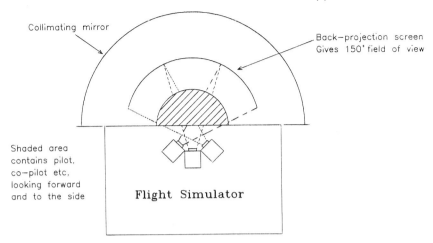

Collimating mirror

Back—projection screen
Gives 150° field of view

Shaded area
contains pilot,
co—pilot etc,
looking forward
and to the side

Flight Simulator

Fig. 5.8 WIDE system

which the computer-generated images are displayed goes beyond even the performance requirements of Phase 3. The purpose of this new display system is to present images to the entire flight deck without optical limitation. The most important part of this display system is an advanced calligraphic projector capable of translating the signals from the image generating computers into high resolution projected pictures. The field of view available using this system is 150° horizontally by 40° vertically.

Figure 5.8 illustrates the main structure of the system. The crew sit in the flight deck mock-up rather like people sitting in a cinema. Calligraphic projectors behind and above them project the computer images on to a screen in front of them. Unlike a flat cinematic screen, this image is projected on to a specially designed back-projection screen. The image so formed is viewed by the occupants of the flight deck from a large-diameter collimating mirror extending around the entire flight deck structure. This system, known as WIDE, can be used with any of Rediffusion's advanced simulators instead of normal CRT modules. One of the simulation systems that can incorporate the WIDE displays is Rediffusion/Sutherland's CT-5 system. This represents the state-of-the-art in simulators and will now be looked at in depth.

(a) CT-5 System

The Continuous Tone CT-5 system provides significantly higher levels of detail, texture and flexibility than any other existing simulator. This increase in performance was largely seen to be of use to combat pilots simulating low-level flying missions. In such situations detail and texture are vital in judging attitude

Fig. 5.9 F-16 jets (courtesy Rediffusion simulation)

and speed. The first installation of a CT-5 system was to a CH-46E helicopter simulator. This particulator simulator has six monitors aimed at the helicopter captain. Five of these monitors are placed in the helicopter windows around the simulator to give a 180° field of view. The sixth is placed outside what is known as the chin window. Plate 5 shows a CH-46 helicopter flying over mountain terrain. One interesting feature to note is that the rotor blades actually rotate at a realistic speed. The ability to display multiple moving objects with moving parts is one of the key features of the CT-5: this is demonstrated in the picture of several F-16 jets in Fig. 5.9.

The CT-5 image generator is not necessarily limited to military training. Other applications include ship handling and engineering development. Boeing Computer Services have installed a CT-5 simulator for 757/767 simulation. This unit was used towards cockpit design but is now also useful for flight-tests and investigation of ground handling in poor weather. Plate 10 is a picture of a Boeing 757 from this system.

Now that the general characteristics of the CT-5 have been outlined it is a valuable exercise to describe the exact structure of this system, how it works, and the departures it makes from conventional simulation techniques.

Figure 5.10 shows the basic configuration of CT-5 components that provide a single channel to drive one monitor. Each component in this configuration is

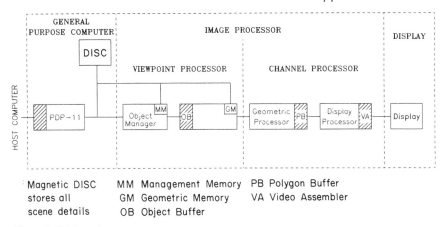

Magnetic DISC — MM Management Memory — PB Polygon Buffer
stores all — GM Geometric Memory — VA Video Assembler
scene details — OB Object Buffer

Fig. 5.10 CT-5 configuration

responsible for a series of tasks that combine to form a completed image approximately 30 times a second. The major components include a general-purpose computer (a Dec PDP-11), special-purpose hardware called an image processor, and a display.

The general-purpose computer is the link between the image processor and the host computer. It manages and monitors the overall visual system and hosts the magnetic disc on which the data-base is stored.

The four components between the PDP-11 and the display itself convert incoming pictorial data into the final image ready for display. Collectively they are known as the image processor. The cross-hatched areas in Fig. 5.10 represent the several field buffer memories in the system. The four elements of the image processor are the object manager, the polygon manager, the geometric processor and the display processor, and work as follows.

(i) Object manager
The object manager has the general task of producing a set of potentially visible scene elements once it is given the eyepoint of the pilot. This involves searching the data-base to extract the least possible number of scene elements from this eyepoint and sorting these into visual priority order (front to back). In order to handle very large numbers of scene elements an extremely efficient data-base structure is essential. This data-base will now be briefly discussed.

The data-base is a hierarchical tree structure of geographically related levels of detail. These details are all the polygons and lights that go to make up simulated landscapes and objects. They are structured so that basic visibility tests are rapid and minimal. The structure can be appreciated by reference to Fig. 5.11.

A definition of terms and processes in Fig. 5.11 will make the structure more apparent:

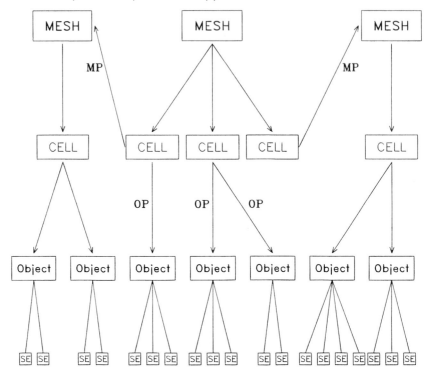

SE Scene element
MP Mesh pointer
OP Object pointer

Fig. 5.11 Display element structure

1. Scene element: these are the lowest levels of detail and are either polygons or lights. Each one can contain information about its reflectance, colour, or, if it is a light, special characteristics (e.g. flashing).
2 Object: at the next level up objects are a collection of scene elements, and like scene elements they can possess extra information (e.g. transparency).
3. Cell: a cell is a volume in model space represented by a decision node in the data-base tree. It can have up to two option pointers and a transition stage which can be used to choose between them. Associated with the cell is suffi-cient geometric information to test (crudely) whether it lies within the current field of view.
4. Option pointer: this is a pointer from a cell to either an object or a mesh. If it points to an object, then the tree structure along this path is finished. If it points to a mesh, then more tree tracing may be done.

5. Mesh: at the highest level a mesh is a collection of cells. Included within the mesh is information which allows the visual-priority ordering of the cells to be accomplished. Performing priority tests in these small mesh modules effectively limits priority interactions to small collections of scene data. This eases any necessary 3-D geometry.

Visibility tests are performed to eliminate, as early as possible and in pieces as large as possible, those portions of the data-base which will not appear in any display channel. Only general tests are carried out by the object manager; critical tests are done in the polygon manager at scene element level.

The data-base tree is the structure of meshes and objects organized by their geographical association into cells. For every single image generated (about 30 per second) the cell processor is given an eyepoint and the data-base mesh pointer. When a mesh is processed the priority processor determines the output order of the cells while the cell processor performs field-of-view and transition-range calculations. Cells which do not appear on any channel are not output. The remaining cells are output in their priority order, and the transition-range calculations are used to determine, for each cell, which option pointer will be used.

The final element of the data-base system is an algorithm (called the Pager) whose function is to manage the physical memory inside the object manager so that potentially required data-base scene elements are resident. If it does not find the necessary elements it requests them from the PDP-11.

(ii) Polygon manager
The polygon manager performs a series of further, far more precise, tests on the elements processed by the object manager and stored in its field buffer memory. These tests are conducted using the geometry memory, which contains the vertex and structural data for scene elements. Those scene elements surviving this series of tests continue to be processed for shading (primarily sun illumination calculations). Each scene element is then output to the geometric processor.

(iii) Geometric processor
The geometric processor receives scene elements (polygons and lights) in model space coordinates from the polygon manager. These polygons are transformed to channel coordinates and clipped against the boundary (window) of the channel. The vertices within the channel boundary are then scaled to the resolution of the screen attached to that channel. The resultant description of all legal scene elements is stored in the polygon buffer to be processed by the display processor.

(iv) Display processor
The display processor completes the operations required to form an actual t.v. image. Figure 5.12 outlines the tasks necessary to accomplish this.

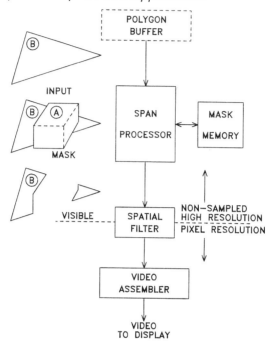

Fig. 5.12 Display processor

The most important facet of the display processor is that it operates on rectangular areas of the screen called spans (collections of display pixels). Most other simulators employ scan-line processing, i.e. analysing the picture one scan-line (a scan-line being one entire horizontal line of pixels on a t.v. screen) at a time. Span processing is rapid and allows higher resolution than scan-line processing.

The sequence of tasks performed by the display processor is as follows:

1. The polygon buffer (containing descriptions of objects in visual-priority order) passes scene elements to the span processor one by one, beginning with the polygon nearest to the eyepoint. The Span processor prepares an analytic description of the scene element within the current span.
2. The mask memory is used to erase the portions of this analytic description which correspond to portions of the span which are already masked.
3. The remainder (in Fig. 5.12 this would be the two sub-polygons formed by polygon A obscuring polygon B) are computed to be visible and can, therefore, be passed to the spatial filter to add to the overall video image of this particular span.

4. The element is shaded and coloured and finally passed to the video assembler memory which takes the red, green and blue components at pixel level and converts this into video output for the display.

5. The analytic description of the geometry of the polygon is then added to the mask memory to help process further scene elements within this span.

Several advantages result from this set of operations. Most important is the high degree of accuracy it implements at the final stage of display. This accuracy is derived from a number of factors. First, the image presented to the spatial filter is a faithful, high resolution rendition of the geometry involved. Second, span processing allows all imagery to be treated identically. Third, spatial filtering retains a good deal of minute picture detail.

The CT-5 system benefits greatly from a coherent, efficient data-base architecture and from a logical subdivision of tasks to dedicated hardware. The display processor in particular ensures that final image quality is highly detailed and flexible. Plates 9, 11 and 12 are all taken from CT-5 systems. There is another approach to simulator displays which is even more novel (if still in its infancy), and which has the promise of even greater flexibility and usefulness. That technology is in helmet-mounted projection.

(b) Helmet-mounted laser projection

Helmet-mounted display systems have been around, in one form or another, for several years. Commonly they have small CRTs on which an image is generated and optics project light into one or both of the pilot's eyes via mirrors or beam splitters located in front of the eyes. This makes them appear like miniature t.v. sets attached to the head. More recent research and development has suggested a very different approach. Redifon in particular have done considerable work towards producing a helmet-mounted laser projector which projects the scene outwards from the pilot's helmet on to a dome screen. The advantages of direct projection from a helmet on to a dome screen are extensive:

1. The display automatically rotates with the head-pointing direction giving an effectively unlimited field of view.

2. High-quality images are possible by projection on to a retro-reflecting screen.

3. Two or more flight crew can use the same simulator cockpit without seeing distorted views of each other's head/eye directed scenes.

4. Using a dome screen provides automatic and precise blanking of the projected outside-world scene at the cockpit outline, since the cockpit structure does not retro-reflect.

5. The entire system should be very cost-effective; only two computer image generation channels are required.

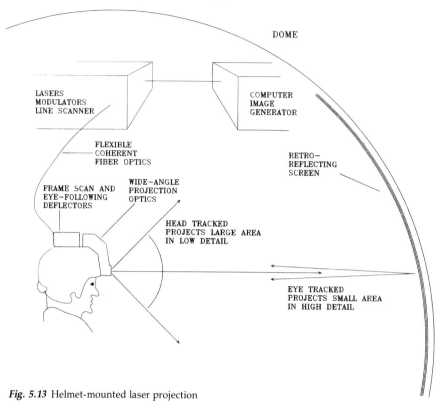

Fig. 5.13 Helmet-mounted laser projection

Figure 5.13 is an illustration of how the system would operate.

The basic premise behind the system depicted in Fig. 5.13 is that the display performance, in terms of field of view and resolution, is matched to the visual performance of the pilot's eyes. This is because the human eye can only perceive high detail at any instant in a relatively small area. So only two sets of images are actually required. One is a narrow projection containing high detail (corresponding to the area being looked at directly by the eyes), the second is a much wider image, far less detailed, dictated by the head position. In Fig. 5.13 the pilot has all the projection apparatus actually on top of his helmet. In order to achieve high, clear brightness over a wide angle a laser display system and an integrated fibre optic link to carry light to the helmet are essential. Lasers allow high brightness across a wide field and the flexible fibre link permits heavy optical components to be mounted away from the helmet. The fibre link itself is more viable because of a light-weight frame scanner on the helmet. This means that the optical fibres are required to transmit line images, rather than full-frame images.

The screen itself is a spherical dome surrounding the simulator cockpit, giving the pilot a field of view limited only by the cockpit structure. The screen is coated with a retro-reflecting material to make the projected image as bright and crisp as possible. In order to focus the pilot's eyes on this bright image the cockpit structure itself is made of non-reflecting material, to avoid moving images falling on the cockpit.

There are still problems in providing a fully working and efficient system. These development problems include producing a high-specification reflective material, selection and processing of two very different levels of detail simultaneously and, by far the most difficult problem, building head-tracking and eye-tracking instruments that are efficient and do not make the pilot feel uncomfortable or unnatural. Once these areas are resolved then helmet projection systems will offer high resolution, wide angles, and more natural simulation at a very reasonable cost.

5.4 MISCELLANEOUS

Other areas in science and industry in which computer graphics plays an important role are numerous and complex. They include applications ranging from the design of a shoe to the design of an entire ship or aircraft, and as diverse as tracking an invisible sub-atomic particle or producing a re-creation of the evolution of our galaxy. To treat them all in any kind of depth would require a book too heavy to hold, and far too long to read, therefore this section will conclude with a brief summary of three more of these areas before moving on to look at applications where the picture is more important than the data itself.

5.4.1 Mapping

Maps are a natural vehicle for presenting geographical information about our environment in order to analyse problems and form solutions. This can extend from undersea oil exploration to urban and regional planning. The data to produce maps can come from digitizing existing maps, processing satellite data, or carrying out field mapping specifically for computer input. The maps themselves can be the simple road types that are familiar to every motorist or, more usefully, thematic and topographical types. Thematic maps are commonly used in translating statistics about an area into a visual form. The most common type of thematic map is the choropleth map. Figures 5.14 and 5.15 are examples of such maps. They can be used to present information about land use, taxation, farming methods, distribution of essential services, in fact anything for which there are available statistics.

Topographical maps are used to present a 3-D view of an area displaying various data (e.g. the presence of minerals or resources) and accurately describing the topology of that area. To help in determining the most informa-

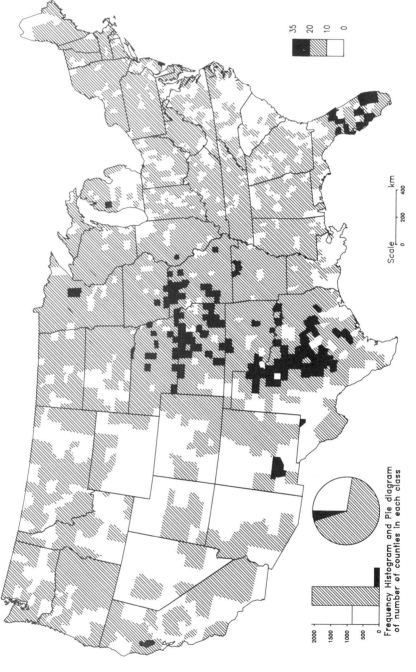

Fig. 5.14 United States of America: percentage of people aged 65 years and over. Compiled on GIMMS by A.W. Carruthers and T.C. Waugh (source: *The County and City Databook, 197*: Washington, 197.)

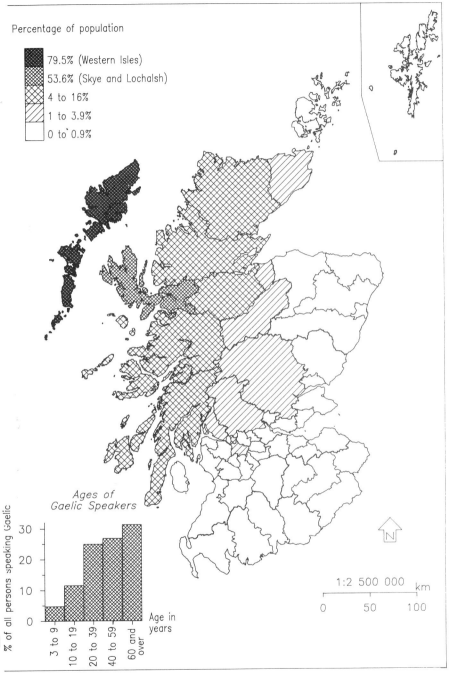

Fig. 5.15 Gaelic speakers 1981 aged 3 years and over (population resident on Census night). Compiled on GIMMS by A.W. Carruthers and T.C. Waugh (Crown Copyright, S.D.D., 1983)

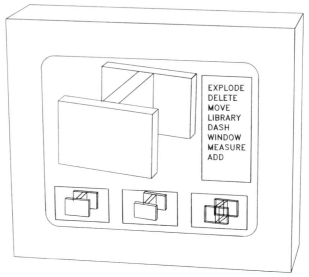

EXPLODE
DELETE
MOVE
LIBRARY
DASH
WINDOW
MEASURE
ADD

Fig. 5.16 Typical CAD station

tive viewing angle the viewpoint can be continually changed. Plate 1 is a perspective view of part of Greenland.

5.4.2 Computer-aided design (CAD)

Computer-aided design is something of a catch-all term for a very wide range of graphic activities. It has been around since the earliest days of computer graphics but is currently witnessing an ever-increasing rate of growth. Defining it can be very tricky but broadly speaking it involves using a computer to aid in any of the design stages of a product, the product itself being anything between a shelf-bracket and a Boeing 747. Those industries already employing CAD include mechanical engineering, architecture, bio-chemistry, printed circuit board design, textiles, and the earliest users, the motor car and aerospace industries.

The advantages of designing on a graphic display vary greatly between products, but at base the computer is most useful when tackling either very repetitive designs or very complex ones. Small components can be reproduced instantly wherever needed, and subtle or major changes can be made to existing designs. Interactive systems, particularly, result in draughtsmen being able to evaluate large numbers of possible options before choosing the optimum design. This frequently has the added benefit of doing away with the need to build experimental equipment. Figure 5.15 is taken from a simple interactive program that allows a machine part to be created, modified and analysed (weight, volume, reaction to heat and stress, etc.). Often the design stage can be incorporated into a complete process so that the data generated by the design can be fed (via some form of numerical control) to operate the machine cutting tools that actually make the product. To help further in this process solid modelling systems have become very popular in forming near photographic images of products before they are even made. Plate 2 shows one such example.

5.4.3 Chemistry

The use of computers in chemistry has for many years been very very extensive, and in particular interactive graphics has proved extremely useful both in education and industry. In the classroom it can be used to help students with the interpretation and significance of ideas which are difficult to visualize from a conventional textbook or blackboard tutorial. Probably its most impressive usage, in academic and industrial research, is in simulation (or modelling). Here it can be used to give researchers large numbers of views of molecular structures. Plates 13 and 14 are two computer images of the results of an extensive program of research, carried out by ICI, into the design of a commercial fungicide. In this example molecular modelling was used to optimize the design of a substrate molecule which, by blocking an enzyme, could be used to destroy the fungus. A complete examination of the enzyme structure, helped by systematic computer visualizations, resulted in the theoretical fungicide proving spectacularly successful once synthesized and tested. Plate 15 shows a fully shaded image of the molecular interaction, and plate 14 is a more usual ball-and-stick representation of this interaction. The use of colour coding in both these types of representation allows easy identification while the effects of shadow and light in Plate 15 give the researcher a realistic idea of the 3-D structure of the molecules without the need to construct physical models. Figure 5.17 shows similar view plotted on an ordinary drum plotter.

5.5 PROJECTS

1. Write an interactive program to accept data and titles for display as pie charts. Include as many facilities such as keys, segment shading, and segment labelling, as possible.
2. The time is not too far away when office and home computer systems will offer powerful and versatile software packages in the computer-aided design area. What functions would you include in a general-purpose CAD package? How interactive would it be and what hard-copy devices would be practical?
3. Besides the maritime and aviation industries, who else might benefit from the use of simulators? Choose one in particular and try to specify how the simulator might work and what it would do.
4. Three-dimensional histograms are often used to display complex statistics

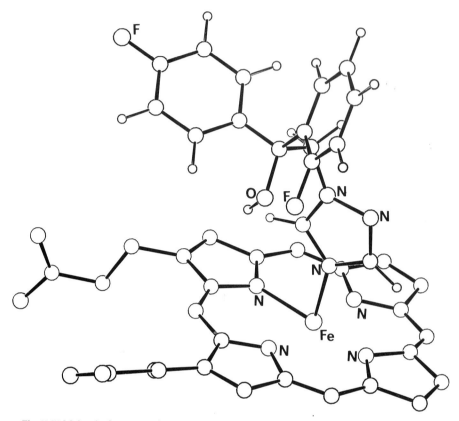

Fig. 5.17 Molecule drawn on plotter

(e.g. the annual growth rates of several cities over a period of years). Write the code to produce such a histogram including axis-labelling and hidden-line removal.

5. In mapping software it is often very useful to be able to automatically draw sets of smooth, parallel lines to represent features such as railway tracks, canals and bus routes. Write the code to take a set of points and generate such lines.

6. Small computer systems are increasingly being used by medical practices. Choose one specific area and write a program to classify and display data pertinent to that area. An example would be a dental practice. Here it would be useful to keep a patient's record on a PET, APPLE, or similar microcomputer so that the record could be retrieved and a dental picture displayed. Previous work done and fillings, etc. still required could be appropriately highlighted.

6

Art and animation

This chapter will attempt to describe and discuss those uses of computer graphics which can be felt, intuitively, to be artistic in nature rather than scientific. Often this tends to be an area much neglected by the computer media, but its impact on people is far more widespread than any of the applications described in the previous chapter.

6.1 GRAPHIC DESIGN

Of all the areas that could be included in this chapter perhaps the fastest growing is commercial graphic design. The traditional task of the graphic designer has been to produce slides, transparencies, pictures for books and magazines, posters for billboards and exhibitions, and stills for t.v. and film. To accomplish this successfully requires more than just proficient draughting skills. It demands the ability to present facts and figures in a visually interesting way, and to convey ideas as descriptively, and convincingly, as possible. These objectives apply even more keenly to pictures generated by a computer where it is all too easy to produce a graph or image that is garish, difficult to understand, or just plain boring. The experience and training of the graphic designer provide guidelines to compose pictures successfully. In Fig. 6.1, for instance, a number of simple features help to make what is basically a histogram both interesting and informative. Instead of plain bars images pertinent to the product are used (in this case bricks). Typefaces are kept simple, smooth and uncluttered (nothing is more distracting than several typefaces all jostling with each other) so that the information is legible. Finally a simple border pulls the whole thing together. Such straightforward details seem obvious but are actually very dificult to master. Even more critical is the way in which colour is used. It is very easy to produce pictures where the eye wanders around trying to avoid bright reds on a blue background, or the important piece of information is lost in a spaghetti of coloured blocks and curly typefaces. Here again a few simple guidelines can help to produce a successful picture: emphasize a polygon by giving it a coloured edge; avoid blue on a black background; use soft, neutral backgrounds to allow coloured bars or logos to stand out; use colours of similar hue. All this knowledge and technique can be applied to computer graphics systems. All that is required of the designer is the willingness to try a totally

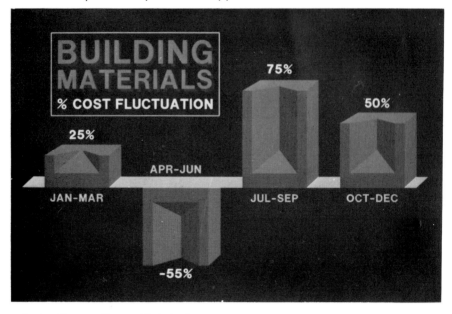

Fig. 6.1 (Courtesy Concept Marketing)

new way of achieving the same goals.

What benefits can using a computer system bring to the graphic artist? Primarily it offers two advantages: more pictures in less time, and effects that would be extremely difficult and costly to do any other way. To illustrate these advantages and the facilities offered by advanced video systems the Digital Paint Box (produced by Quantel) will be examined in more detail.

6.2 THE VIDEO ARTIST

Video and slide production are by far the most dynamic areas in which computers are helping graphic designers. Typical of the stand-alone graphic systems currently available at the higher end of the market is the Paint Box System. This attempts to provide a designer with all the colours, brushes, scissors, glue, rulers and typefaces that would be available in an ordinary office environment. The only real difference is that they are electronic, but they respond to the artist as easily and sensitively as anything made of wood or metal.

One of the knottiest problems with systems designed for graphic artists is how they actually input a picture and then react with that picture. In some systems images can be drawn directly on special touch-sensitive screens, in others mice and joysticks are used to control the pen position (i.e. the cursor) on the display. By far the most popular method, however, is a digitizer (also referred to as a 'touch tablet') and some form of stylus. The stylus used on the Paint Box is a highly sensitive pen that answers to the pressure of the hand, making the painting process feel more natural. It is the versatility of this electronic brush which expands the freedom and speed of the professional graphic artist. In the Paint Box it can be instantly changed to one of five different modes. These modes, or variations on them, are found on most top-range video-image systems. In the Paint Box they are:

1. Paint: this is the basic method of drawing and most closely resembles traditional oils in appearance. To provide more realistic control the stylus will deposit the colour on the screen thinly if little pressure is used, or thickly (making the new colour opaque) if more pressure is put on the stylus.
2. Wash: as the name suggests this mode results in an effect rather like conventional water colours. The pixels on the screen remain translucent so that underlying detail is never quite lost.
3. Shade: this is more or less the opposite to Wash. The tonal range is strictly controlled, making it ideal for tinting and shading areas.
4. Chalk: this mode adds a gritty texture to the brush strokes, giving a feeling of depth and solidity; the result is very much like using chalk or crayon.
5. Air brush: one of the most popular features with artists and designers. This mode mimics a real air-brush; paint is deposited as a spray of fine dots (pixels within the area of the stylus are sampled and a number of them are coloured). It is an ideal tool to produce the softness required to pick out clouds on a weather map, blowing hair, or the change of texture on a billowing flag.

Besides the type of paint selected the artist can also choose a pen size ranging from a fine tip to a wide brush. The ships and flag in Fig. 6.2 and the tropical island in Plate 16 were both painted using a variety of these paints and brush sizes.

Other facilities available in the Paint Box include being able to magnify a particular section of an image (in order to add fine details) and to use an electronic pair of scissors together with invisible glue to cut, re-size, fuse, rotate and move pictures anywhere on the screen. This is very useful when added to another simple but powerful feature of the Paint Box. Like several other systems it can accept live video input. This allows t.v. pictures to be frozen and then used like any other picture. As a frozen t.v. image is no more than a collection of RGB values for each pixel in the digital video memory (like the squirrel in Plate 17) the same colours present in the picture can be used for precise re-touching, additional graphics, or inserting various types of text.

An important area in computer graphics which has only recently begun to be explored in any real depth is the generation of professional fonts. Traditionally most people working in installations with plotters and displays were restricted to a very similar set of typefaces (often only one) with little control over charac-

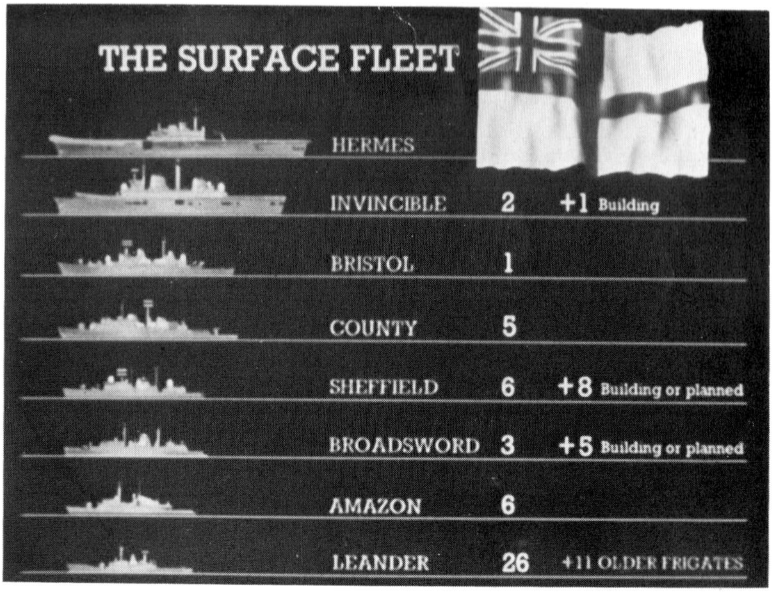

THE SURFACE FLEET			
HERMES			
INVINCIBLE	2	+1 Building	
BRISTOL	1		
COUNTY	5		
SHEFFIELD	6	+8 Building or planned	
BROADSWORD	3	+5 Building or planned	
AMAZON	6		
LEANDER	26	+11 OLDER FRIGATES	

Fig. 6.2 (Courtesy Quantel Limited)

ter spacing or positioning. Further, because such typefaces were defined as sets of vectors, once they were enlarged beyond a certain size their appearance was more like that of a skeleton than a character. Some methods were developed to solidify these typefaces (Appendix 2 discusses these) but they remained limited in their usefulness. Systems such as the Paint Box, however, can offer versatile and professional fonts to the standard required by t.v. commercials, publicity advertisements, or magazine publication. Using the Paint Box any of a wide range of fonts can be selected, altered to any size or colour, given automatic proportional spacing, and then special effects such as drop shadow and blind embossing can be added to convey a solid 3-D effect. Figure 6.3 is an example of these fonts and effects.

6.3 ANIMATION

Of all the uses that computers can be put to probably the most interesting, exciting and challenging to graphic artists is in the field of animation. From t.v. commercials to major Hollywood blockbusters it is used to produce highly distinctive images that can intrigue, impress and dazzle the viewer. These images can be generated by a variety of techniques which, for simplicity, can be subdivided into two broad categories: traditional 2-D animation and full 3-D computer imaging.

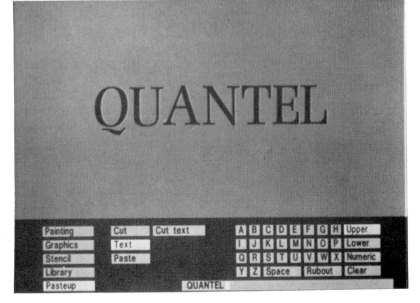

Fig. 6.3 (Courtesy Quantel Limited)

6.3.1 2-D animation

The kind of animation familiar to generations of film and t.v. audiences is the type of cartoon film produced by studios such as Walt Disney. These cartoons were, and are, expensive to produce because the processes involved are painstaking and extremely labour-intensive. These processes follow a well-defined sequence of steps:

1. A storyboard is agreed which outlines all the events in the film.
2. A soundtrack is recorded.
3. This soundtrack is broken down into minute sections. This is especially important for sound effects such as doors slamming and characters speaking. Animators can then know the precise frame in which to match lip movements, etc. to sound.
4. The most important frames (known as key frames) which describe the action are drawn by the main animators.
5. The frames in between these are drawn by assistants.
6. All drawings are transferred to celluloid and coloured in by hand.
7. Everything is checked and final editing completed.

To help in the stages outlined above computers are useful in two ways. One, they can be used to produce each individual frame by mimicking the techniques of conventional animation. Two, a variety of the more time-consuming and laborious tasks can be performed automatically. These include producing the transitional frames (step 5) and colouring in (step 6).

(a) Following traditional methods

In the past the basic mechanism to produce a 3-D effect in cartoons has been to overlay two or more flat pictures on top of each other. Slight movement of these top layers results in the impression of animated movement. At the simplest level this can mean merely moving one foreground picture over a static background. Figure 6.4 is an example of this straightforward method applied to a t.v. weather chart. Several clouds 'painted' with a Paint Box air-brush are positioned over a stationary picture of Great Britain and are stored as separate video images. When played back in sequence the effect is of a bank of clouds moving from the sea to cover the land.

Taking this process further a series of picture layers can be drawn and stored in a digital library (most frequently on some form of hard disc) and then manipulated to provide a much more realistic impression of 3-D movement. This manipulation would work as follows:

One picture is transferred from the digital library and displayed as a fixed background. A second picture can then be called up and drawn over the top of this to provide a foreground. Other shapes are able to move between these layers. In fact, several foreground layers can be defined, all that needs to be

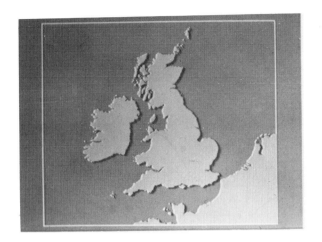

Fig. 6.4 (Courtesy Quantel Limited)

Fig. 6.5 (Courtesy Quantel Limited)

ensured is that they are drawn in the correct sequence. The squirrel in Fig. 6.5 is shown moving between only two layers (a background and one foreground), but the final result is an acceptable colourful picture of a squirrel strolling through the woods munching nuts. To produce an even more convincing impression of depth each individual frame could be drawn completely from scratch. The perspective of the background, shapes, and foreground could be made to change in relation to each other. However, this would be very time consuming.

(b) Computer-assisted animation

Computers can be used to actually assist the process of animation in several ways. One is by filling in polygons using a predetermined colour or brush. This is useful in two ways. First, it helps to replace the repetitive task of hand-colouring pictures on celluloid. Second, some video-image systems allow the artist to define patterns as a brush type; this facilitates extremely rapid picture creation and colouring. For instance a cluster of leaves can be specified as the brush type allowing trees, hedges and plants to be drawn in detail by simply moving the stylus around. This process can be extended to create a library of texture types (or patterns). Thus polygons can be filled in automatically with various patterns such as bricks and grass.

A second process which can be performed by the computer is the generation of transitional frames. This is more widely known as 'inbetweening' and has undergone a great deal of research and development. The basic task can be easily defined: given two pictures, generate one or more pictures part way between them. If animation of a very simple type is required the solution is a straightforward one of interpolation. In Fig. 6.6 the dragon can be made to raise its leg in any given number of steps. All that is required is a starting frame (a) and a closing frame (i). The difference between each (X, Y) coordinate of these two frames can then be subdivided into any number of stages. Where coordinates remain the same (i.e. in the rest of the dragon's body) there is no difference, so the intermediate (X, Y) coordinate will remain the same. Figure 6.7 is a very simple routine which will calculate any number of intermediate steps between two coordinates, and was used to produce frames (b) to (h) in Fig. 6.6.

This simplest form of interpolation requires that both pictures are drawn with the same number of lines and with only continuously visible movements. Unfortunately in most animation any two key frames will involve some part of a body or object becoming invisible. Even if a character turns only slightly between two frames part of the head, shoulder, arms or legs will become obscured. For an animator this is second nature because what is actually being drawn is a 2-D projection of a 3-D image in the artist's head. It is not second nature to the computer. To accomplish inbetweening correctly it must be given information about how different sections of a body can move in front of, or

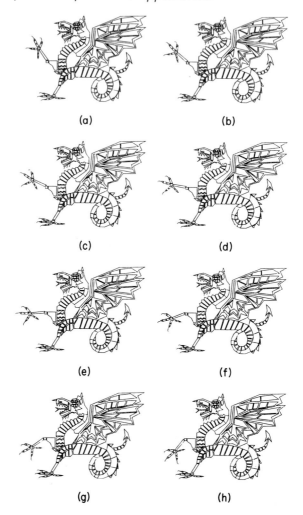

(a)   (b)

(c)   (d)

(e)   (f)

(g)   (h)

Fig. 6.6 Simple 'inbetweening'

behind, other sections. This is not easy. Of the various approaches that have been tried one of the earliest and most promising was to first model the character with a wire-frame skeleton. The computer could be given sufficient information about the mechanics of this skeleton (limb rotation, etc.) to compute inbetween frames requiring only slight re-touching. The current trend however is towards animating objects, including the human body, using solid-modelling techniques. This will be discussed under 3-D computer imaging.

ROUTINE BETWEEN (NSTEPS, XFIRST, YFIRST, XLAST, YLAST)

{ (XFIRST, YFIRST) is any vector on (a)
  (XLAST, YLAST) is the corresponding vector on (i) }

XDIFF = XLAST−XFIRST
YDIFF = YLAST−YFIRST
XSTEP = XDIFF/NSTEPS
YSTEP =YDIFF/NSTEPS

{ Compute NSTEPS number of intermediate vectors, these can be drawn or stored }

FOR I: = TO NSTEPS DO

      BEGIN
      X = XFIRST + (XSTEP $_*$ I)
      Y = YFIRST + (YSTEP $_*$ I)
      END

Fig. 6.7 Simple routine

(c) Colour-table animation

A quite novel method of producing animated effects on colour terminals is by manipulation of the colour table. This table contains the RGB values of all the colours that can be seen at any one time on the display screen. So a terminal that can, for instance, display up to 16 colours may actually have sufficient memory in its colour table to allow each of these colours to be a mixture of 16 levels each of red, green and blue. Figure 6.8 is a desert island scene which is animated in a variety of ways using the colour table. Birds fly, clouds roll across the sky, the sun sinks, night falls and the moon rises. The techniques to accomplish this are simple and rely only on changing the RGB values in the colour table. The method is to draw the scene and the desired sequence of movements all in one picture, but to define the colour of these movements to be identical to the background surrounding them. Thus in Fig. 6.8 several sets of birds were drawn but only one set was specified in a visible colour. Making the birds appear to move required the following steps:

1. Change the colour of the first, visible, set of birds to the background colour.
2. Define the colour of the second set to be visible.
3. Change this second set to be invisible again.
4. Define the colour of the third set to be visible.
5. Continue this sequence of steps until only the last set of birds is visible.

The limitation of this method is that it leads to a jerky type of animation. A smoother movement is possible by rippling an object. This involves first drawing a shape as a series of connected segments and then rippling through it,

Fig. 6.8 (Courtesy Alistair Austen)

switching colours off and on. The clouds in Fig. 6.8 were made to roll by using this method. Figure 6.9 illustrates exactly what happens to one cloud. The other clouds, all drawn in an equal number of segments and in the same sequel of colours, also appear to be in motion at the same time.

1. Segments 1 to 6 all visible.
2. Segment 1 turned to background colour, segment 7 turned to cloud colour.
3. Segment 2 turned to background colour, segment 8 turned to cloud colour.
4. This process repeated until segments 1 to 6 are all in the background colour and segments 7 to 12 are all visible.

Colour-table animation is a straightforward process that lends itself to all manner of tricks by inventive artists. It can be used to create sequences demonstrating the principles of magnetism, how machines work, how satellites orbit planets or just clouds floating over an island in the sun. Whatever the use, video tables are a relatively easy method of producing short, effective pieces of animation. Producing something more, something that looks and behaves as if it were part of a real world, requires using 3-D animation.

6.3.2 3-D animation

The most sophisticated and impressive use of computer graphics by the film-maker is in the production of images that can be manipulated in three

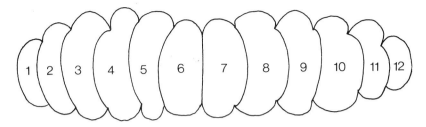

Fig. 6.9 Colour-table rippling

dimensions. This is similar in many respects to the simulators described in Chapter 5 but the needs of t.v. and film tend to require more intricate and glossy images. Whereas simulators confine themselves to relatively simple objects that can be displayed in real-time the film-maker demands short, highly-detailed sequences that may include very complex objects. Producing such high quality pictures can be achieved using wire-frame animation or by employing solid-modelling and shading techniques to create both a complete environment and its inhabitants.

(a) Wire-frame animation

The use of pure outlines to describe objects has been used for many years in a variety of graphic applications. As a technique it is well understood, straightforward to program and has two useful advantages over surface-shaded images. First, processing time is kept significantly smaller because no complex raster shading algorithms are required. Second, the final picture can be displayed on any type of graphic v.d.u. or plotter. This versatility has made it a popular tool to the animator for many years. Today its most widespread uses in the film industry are in producing t.v. commercials and progam title sequences, both of which require short but striking images.

Using wire-frame animation to create unusual and effective picture sequences requires the imagination and experience of the animator, together with as many software facilities as possible. One of the problems of using computer graphics to produce animated scenes is in providing a natural, easy interface between computer and animator. To overcome this problem many modern computer film companies have systems which are made to include virtually all of the features of a motion camera in a film studio. For instance in Fig. 6.10 the camera zooms in on the city while continually twisting the view-point. When the street level is reached the camera straightens out and a video glow is added to the street lights. In Fig. 6.11 (a title sequence) this technique is stretched even further. The camera hurtles through a curving tunnel until the final title literally bursts up into view. The Nikon commercial illustrated in Fig.

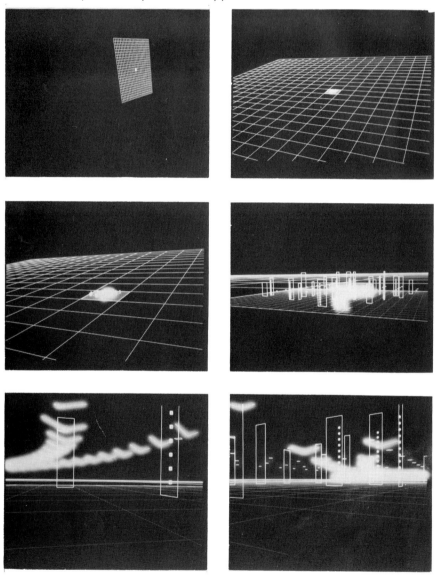

Fig. 6.10 (Courtesy The Moving Picture Company)

6.12 adopts a simpler mechanism of building up detail in time to a changing angle until a complete 35 mm camera faces the viewer. Many other special effects can be included in wire-frame scenes and often the computer sequence is mixed with live footage or is hand-coloured, but as more features are added to these systems it becomes increasingly economic to abandon wire-frame

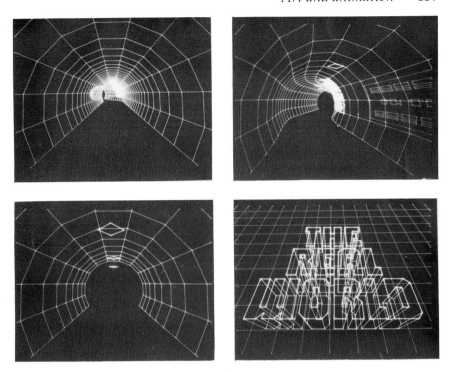

Fig. 6.11 (Courtesy The Moving Picture Company)

modelling and take the next step into full computer imaging.

(b) Computer imaging

The increasing refinement of surface-modelling techniques and the large-scale dissemination of algorithms to generate reflections, shadows and textures has resulted in an explosion of companies offering computer-image animation. This is especially true in the United States, where companies such as Magi Synthevision, Digital Productions, and III have been producing computer-imaged sequences for films and t.v. for several years. All three were involved in generating the computer imagery for Disney's film *TRON*. One film-maker (George Lucas of *Star Wars* fame) has even set up a unit devoted entirely to computer graphics research. The team in this unit have developed some fascinating and useful modelling methods. Elsewhere, in England and in mainland Europe, companies have sprung up to produce solid image sequences for t.v. commercials and programs. All these companies are able to offer a type and complexity of animation that would be extremely difficult, if not impossible, to produce by the artist's hand. The advantages, versatility and scope of such animation can be summarized as follows:

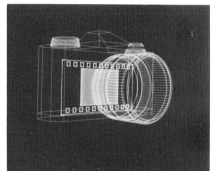

Fig. 6.12 (Courtesy The Moving Picture Company)

1. A complete environment can be constructed and objects moved within it. Background features such as mountains, lakes, buildings, sky and trees can all be specified to a minute level of detail. When a change in the viewpoint is required the perspective of all these details can be re-calculated and displayed. Objects ranging from cars to spaceships can be programmed to move through a computer-imaged landscape and shadows, changes in lighting and coloration can be continually updated.

2. Objects can be drawn that are extremely difficult to illustrate manually, or in some cases even to visualize. These include mathematical concepts, microscopic structures, or vast astronomical events. For example, atoms and molecules can be animated according to predetermined physical laws, calculus can be shown actually happening, and animal or physical processes of evolution can be illustrated in action. In all these cases objects and events can be defined mathematically and the computer used to give life and physical reality.

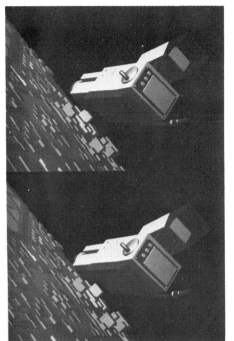 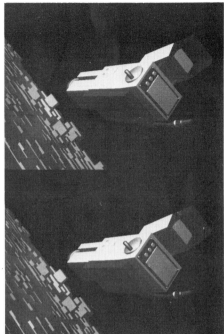

Fig. 6.13 (Courtesy Electronic Arts)

3. Several of the subtle techniques and laborious tasks of the animator can be performed automatically. The problem of inbetweening for instance does not arise because the computer possesses the algorithms to handle 3-D objects and display only visible surfaces. If the reflectivity, colour and surface type of each object is defined in the data-base then the computer can also be left to colour in each frame. This can even include shadows lengthening as the sun descends. Another important technique is accurate control of motion. In real life people and objects do not start, move and stop at one constant speed. There is always a period of slow acceleration and deceleration. These kinds of motion variable can be explicitly specified. Finally, as in wire-frame animation, the image animator can call on standard camera facilities (e.g. zoom, pan, twist, scroll). In Fig. 6.13 a sequence of images from a sports program introduction show a computer camera spinning through space as the real camera viewpoint continually changes. Plates 18 and 19 illustrate another popular and impressive technique of solid-model animation. Because objects are defined mathematically in sections, they can be made to fly apart or come together to form a whole.
4. Every year sees new methods of modelling objects and processes. This

includes such things as subtle types of texture, artificial techniques to generate natural-looking objects (e.g. fractals), and attempts to model extremely complex processes. For instance Lucasfilm (the unit established by George Lucas) have evolved a method for modelling natural processes such as clouds and fire by using particle systems. The use of particles (instead of complex polyhedra) allows dynamic control of motion, expansion, and change.

5. Perhaps the most interesting facet of computer imaging is the attempt to model and animate one of the most familiar, but most complex collections of polyhedra we know — the human body. It is not just the film animator who is interested in producing a realistic moving version of this object — there are other disciplines equally interested in a faithful copy. A computer human can be used to study how the body responds· to closed environments such as cockpits, to help teaching and research in medicine, even to aid choreographers plan and simulate dance movements. It is hardly surprising, therefore, that a great amount of research has been carried out into modelling the human body. The problems involved in this modelling centre on the construction of the body itself and the complex mechanisms by which it moves.

The body is composed of a large number of hinges overlaid by a network of very pliable muscles and skin tissue. Various patches (such as the eyes, ears and hair) are extremely difficult to represent by traditional means. Over the last decade several methods of modelling the basic structure of the body have been produced. Stick-figure representations were popular because they lent themselves to real-time manipulation. More recently circles and ellipsoids have been used to represent the body. Current techniques attempt to use solid image algorithms to reproduce the exact shape and texture of the head and body. One very promising and realistic approach has been developed by the New York Institute of Technology (NYIT). This institute is at the forefront of computer animation research and has carried out a great deal of work into animating the human body and especially the face. One method employed is to parametize the entire face and produce a final image using shaded surfaces. Thus an animator need only specify a set of parameters to construct a particular expression.

There remain many problems in creating fully shaded animation sequences. Inputting 3-D data can be complicated and time consuming; unfortunately (at least for the programmer) not everything in nature is conveniently composed of cubes, prisms and perfect arcs. Besides the actual difficulty of getting 3-D data into the computer the actual modelling algorithm often has to be re-invented for every new type of image to be animated. If a sequence required a seagull flying overhead the anatomy and motion mechanics of a real seagull would have to be carefully analysed and the correct model evolved. Finally, even if the data and modelling is straightforward the amount of computer processing can be extensive. Most companies use film recorders to produce the frames (typically about 24 per second) needed for animation. Each point on every one of these frames has to be individually computed. For t.v. work the normal resolution is about 1000 by 700 points but cinematic film can require much higher resolution. This enormity of calculations necessitates at least a large, dedicated minicomputer.

Leaving these problems to one side computer animation techniques are fast widening the scope and speed of many modern animators. Nevertheless, no computer on today's market is capable of making even the smallest decision about what is effective, creative, or innovative. That is strictly the province of the person in front of the machine. What the computer is doing, however, is opening up exciting horizons for what is possible. After all, animation is, for the computer, a natural function. If the final image transferred to film lacks the life and sparkle of hand-drawn cells that is the fault of the user.

6.4 PROJECTS

1. Produce what you think is a professional looking histogram displaying anything you like (within reason!) Remember the simple guidelines outlined at the beginning of this chapter and try to parametize as many features as you can.
2. Look at the literature on inbetweening in character animation. Write an appreciation of the different methods, specify the basic problems and try to define how you would tackle the problem.
3. Many critics think that the use of computer graphics in advertising and films is beginning to lose its novelty and appeal. What do you think? What new avenues are still waiting to be explored?
4. If you have access to a colour terminal write a simple game incorporating colour-table animation. In maze-type games particularly this method of simulating movement can be used to great effect.
5. Invent a simple cartoon character and write a program to allow it to be moved between different foregrounds and backgrounds. Include a method of colouring in various parts of the character and of changing facial expressions.
6. Design a font (e.g. Tudor or Italic) using the spline points method outlined in Appendix 2. Allow the user to scale the characters as he wishes and provide a facility to fill in the characters.

7

Microcomputer case studies

The applications discussed in the preceding two chapters revolved around fairly expensive computer systems, but microcomputer systems are becoming increasingly powerful and versatile. In particular, many small systems are beginning to offer the range of colours, screen resolution and hardware facilities (e.g. arc drawing and polygon fill) that have hitherto been available only on much more expensive machines. In parallel with these advances many manufacturers are producing expensive input and output devices (vector plotters, mice, 'touch tablets') which can easily attach to a wide range of microcomputers. This trend will continue until home computer systems will have the capability to become graphic work stations in their own right.

This chapter will look at four programs that are ideal to run on microcomputers. Unfortunately most current literature on microcomputer graphics tends to be oriented towards one particular machine and its own implementation of BASIC. Only one example in this chapter is either device or language specific. The other examples are limited to describing principles and possible methods of approach. It is hoped the examples chosen will illustrate the wide range of uses to which microcomputer graphics can be put, and indicate some of the simple techniques in writing such programs.

7.1 GAMES

Without doubt there is one area of computer graphics with which virtually everyone is familiar — video games. The sound and sight of these are evident on every home computer and in every arcade. Their fascination lies in a mixture of bright changing colours, simple electronic sounds, and an instant response to buttons, joysticks, and trackballs. Plate 21 is taken from a game called 'BAR' that relies not on reflexes to shoot aliens or avoid capture, but on the setting of traditional games in a computer graphics environment. A brief look at this particular example will help to illustrate how a modular approach can make computer games more flexible.

The objective of BAR is to provide a range of familiar games in a friendly setting, against a clever, realistic opponent. The games chosen were chess, backgammon, poker, and shut-the-box. The friendly setting just had to be a conventional English pub, and the opponent a wily, if alcoholic, computer.

Fig. 7.1 (Courtesy Judi John)

Once the stage was decided the program became straightforward.

The first task in designing and programming BAR was in the actual picture the user would see. The picture finally decided was chosen because it provides an interesting and lifelike background with sufficient area to display the selected game in reasonable detail.

Figure 7.1 is a plot of the original drawing. In this example a digitizer was used to enter the drawing into the machine. For microcomputers (without an available input device) it would be necessary to draw the picture on graph paper, work out the X, Y coordinates for each line, and enter these as data to the program. Once the scene is defined as a series of coordinates it can be drawn and coloured in. To colour in the scene efficiently this picture was carefully digitized not just as a collection of lines, but as a series of polygons. These polygons were drawn one by one and coloured in using a hardware area-fill facility found on almost all colour graphic terminals and on most microcomputers with colour graphics. The technique involves first drawing a closed polygon and then passing an X, Y coordinate within the polygon (known as a 'seed point') to the computer which proceeds to fill the polygon in a colour specified by the program.

Once the background is drawn one of a number of games can be selected. These are like cassette tapes: they have all been drawn to the same size and perspective and can slot in to the table in the bottom right corner of the picture. The game chosen in the colour plate is called shut-the-box. This works by throwing two dice and removing numbers between one and nine accordingly.

Backgammon was chosen as one of the other alternative games because it also requires the throw of two dice.

A breath of life can be added to the game by giving the picture, and the computer opponent, a slice of personality. In the picture very simple animation can be used to give an impression of reality and activity. This includes a steadily decreasing pint of beer, a window that darkens as evening approaches, and a clock ticking away showing the actual time of day. This clock is not digital, but an ordinary wall type, and works by being continually updated by the clock in the computer processor. For instance, when the minute hand needs to move to show the new minute position, the existing minute hand is first redrawn in the same colour as the clock-face (effectively erasing it) and then is redrawn in the new minute position in black. Similar simple animation is used to make the dice spots flash on and off as if it were rolling, a moon rise gently in the evening, and a cloud scurry by in the window.

The final touch is to give the computer the algorithms to play the various games and a personality appropriate to the setting. In BAR the computer can be asked why it made a particular move. The answer can help to teach subtleties about the game to inexperienced players, and show the limits of the algorithms to more experienced ones. Personality comes into play by allowing the computer to grumble about bad dice or cards, and comment about lucky moves or dice by the user. If the game tends to be a bit slow the computer can become steadily more and more drunk (in proportion to the decreasing pint of beer) and begin to make strange, haphazard moves. It can even decide to tip up the table accidently if it is very drunk and about to be beaten. An element of humour helps to retain interest in one-sided games.

7.2 COMPUTER-AIDED LEARNING (CAL)

Computer-aided learning has been around since the early days of computing. It can be used to teach concepts and practical skills, that sometimes require time-consuming individual tuition, or difficult textbook study. The use of graphics in CAL systems can not only add a new dimension but can also be exciting and dynamic. Most CAL programs are directed at science-based studies (learning diffraction in chemistry, or calculus in mathematics, etc.), but with the large increase in home computers more diverse applications are being investigated every day. One particularly interesting example has been developed by Robin Hight in response to a contest sponsored by Johns Hopkins University. This CAL program is intended to help people with defective hearing master the quite difficult art of lip-reading. The entire system has been written to run on a standard APPLE II microcomputer to allow the system to be easily and widely implemented.

The program works by changing the phonetics of a word into a visual picture of lips, tongue and teeth. In all there are 19 distinct phonetic sounds that can be

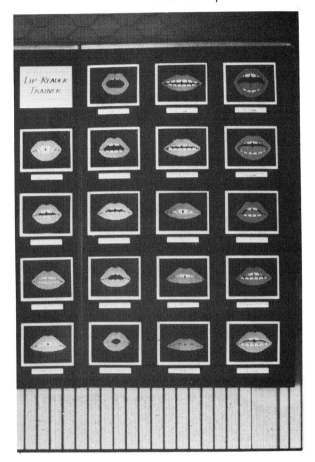

Fig. 7.2 (Courtesy Robin L. Hight)

visually represented in this way. These are shown, taken directly from an
APPLE II display, in Fig. 7.2. The main task of the program is to set up these 19
shapes and convert typed sentences into a corresponding sequence of these
shapes, which may then be controlled by a user to form a complete animated
sentence.

The data necessary to define these shapes, plus the need to actually animate
them, form probably the most frequent problem in programs for microcomputers using graphics — memory. The available memory in a 48k byte APPLE II is
insufficient to handle the disc operating system (DOS), the programs
themselves, and a detailed pixel-by-pixel set of data for each shape. The solution is one commonly used on all sizes of computers. The set of shapes are

broken down into a library of components (like building bricks); these components can then be condensed into tables of data. Whenever an entire shape is required it can be easily and rapidly generated from this data table. The Tibetan alphabet (discussed later) works in a similar way to overcome data size. Using this table the DOS, programs and data can all be loaded into the Apple memory. This leaves the two APPLE graphic pages available for use.

The program uses the principle of video gating (outlined in Chapter 2) to achieve animation. This is produced quite simply. While one mouthshape is displayed on page 1 the second shape is drawn into page 2. Then page 2 is displayed while the third shape is drawn into page 1. This technique gives up to 15 pictures per second, enough for basic animation.

The program itself is divided into three parts. The first allows an instructor to input phonetic sentences in preparation for a training session. To input the sentence 'Please pass the sugar' the following would be typed:

PL>EZ PAS TH@ SH)G@R

Special characters represent a particular enunciation of sound.

The second part is the lip-reader trainer itself. This displays the shapes (the speed of which can be controlled by an APPLE game paddle) and prompts the student to decide what word or sentences have been shown. Figure 7.3 shows a student studying one of the shapes.

Fig. 7.3 (Courtesy Robin L. Hight)

The third part, stores results ready for later analyses. CAL programs such as the 'Lip-reader' are ideal illustrations of how graphics can be used on any size of computer to teach difficult skills or concepts.

7.3 CALLIGRAPHY

In some languages the beauty of the individual characters produces a style of writing that is an art-form in itself. Writing in this style is sometimes known as 'calligraphy' where the sureness and precision of each stroke is as rewarding to produce as it is beautiful to read. The line-drawing displays introduced in Chapter 2 are often referred to as 'calligraphic devices' because they build up pictures from sequences of lines (or 'strokes'). With patience and attention to detail such devices can be made to reproduce intricate and beautiful alphabets faithfully and usefully. One example is a program initially written to produce library catalogue entries for Tibetan texts.   In librarianship, the use of computers for producing catalogue entries is quite common. As, however, the ASCII characters have the shapes of the Roman alphabet, it is necessary to romanize material in languages using other alphabets. This can lead to various problems. In Chinese, for instance, there is more than one way of pronouncing a written symbol and romanization based on one of them will make the entry incomprehensible to users who speak a different form of Chinese, e.g. Cantonese.

Another problem is the absence of one-to-one correspondence between the characters of other alphabets and the Roman one, which leads to several different methods of romanization. An obvious approach to these problems is to write software which can accept ASCII characters and produce a corresponding sequence of characters in another language. This process is known as transliteration. One of the most difficult, but most rewarding, languages to transliterate in this way is Tibetan because in addition to the problem of converting one Tibetan character to a string of Roman characters it also has the problem of grouping characters vertically as well as horizontally. The vertical placement of characters is used in some non-Roman alphabets for vowels, superscripts, or subscripts. In Tibetan each syllable can be composed of several individual elements (e.g. vowels, consonants, subscripts) arranged vertically.

To store each possible syllable would require a large and unwieldy data-base. This program is designed for implementation on a microcomputer where data storage is a critical factor, therefore the program breaks up the vertical column into smaller units. The real donkey work is then done by the program, which accepts ASCII input and reconstructs the correct syllable from a small library of these units. To ensure that the syllable retains a smooth, flowing appearance each individual unit is first blown up from existing master texts and then carefully digitized. When reduced down in size for plotting, imperfections in each syllable are consequently minimized. Figure 7.4 shows the romanized input to the program and the equivalent Tibetan output (produced on a flat-bed plotter).

THE LINES BELOW WERE PRODUCED BY TYPING:

%BLA–MA–LA–SKYABS–SU–MCHI–'AO/
SANGS–RGYAS–LA–SKYABS–SU–MCHI–'AO/
CHOS–LA–SKYABS–SU–MCHI–'AO/––––––––––
DGE–'ADUN–LA–SKYABS–SU–MCHI–'AO#

༄། བླ་མ་ལ་སྐྱབས་སུ་མཆི་འོ། ····

སངས་རྒྱས་ལ་སྐྱབས་སུ་མཆི་འོ། ··

ཆོས་ལ་སྐྱབས་སུ་མཆི་འོ། ········

དགེ་འདུན་ལ་སྐྱབས་སུ་མཆི་འོ།

Fig. 7.4 (Courtesy Sylva Symsova)

The four lines illustrated are taken from a Tibetan prayer.

The overall purpose of this program is to produce a cheap Tibetan word processor. Using graphics to generate the final output means that costly, individualized printers can be easily replaced, and a versatile work station made possible. Such a work station, composed of a microcomputer system and plotter, could be capable of writing in any hand, in any language.

7.4 GRAPHIC HANDICRAFTS

The final area in this chapter can vaguely be described as 'graphic handicrafts'. These cover a vast range of activities which have slowly been growing over the last few years but haven't been explored in any real depth. They revolve around various types of designers (professionals and amateurs) using a computer to help in designing cards, fabrics, japanese fans, jewellery, models, textiles and dozens of other similar products. The main factor distinguishing these applications from commercial CAD is basically the scale involved. In industry, for instance, a fabric can be designed on a v.d.u. and converted into a form suitable to operate the knitting machinery itself. In graphic handicrafts a person uses a computer on an individual level purely for their own work or pleasure. It may be someone creating a quilt cover or a personal stamp album. The basic point is that it is an individual application. This does not preclude it from enjoying the same facilities as large-scale CAD. Ideas, patterns, shapes and designs can be viewed on a screen and repeated, rotated, stretched, squashed and coloured in to the whim of the user. To illustrate these kinds of use, a program to help design Fair-Isle jerseys has been chosen as an example.

Fair-Isle jerseys, traditionally produced in islands off the north coast of Scotland, are knitted in designs which are sometimes said to be Moorish in origin. Such designs rely heavily on interrelated geometric patterns and complex colour schemes, making them difficult to design and especially difficult to visualize. A simple program, called 'Fairisle', was written to perform two simple functions: to make the patterns easy to define, and to help in the selection of a colour scheme. Figure 7.5 shows the method by which this program works. The first problem is to define a single stitch.

Most raster graphic displays and home computers allow a user to define a set of graphic characters which can be positioned to simulate simple graphics. These graphic characters are specified in exactly the same way as the ordinary ASCII characters. An individual stitch can be represented easily and successfully by a shape very similar to a V. Figure 7.5 (a) shows this stitch shape defined in terms of a 7 × 9 character matrix. Once embedded as a graphic character this shape can be positioned and repeated very quickly. Part (b) demonstrates how these stitches are made to interlock to give a more realistic appearance of a piece of knitting. The characters are positioned next to each other horizontally, as if writing ordinary text, but when drawn on the next line up they are positioned lower than normal so that the bottom of the V fits into the top of the V underneath.

The second problem is to specify how these stitches will be put together to form the final knitting pattern. This breaks down into two stages. The first is to define the overall pattern system. This is fairly straightforward. The classic Fair-Isle jersey is constructed from a mesh of diamond shapes (c). This makes knitting the jersey very much easier. The second stage is to specify the pattern within each diamond. Simple Fair-Isle jerseys contain two diamond patterns repeated alternately along one row. This row is then repeated throughout the entire jersey. More complex patterns are achieved by varying the diamond patterns themselves. Plate 22 shows the program displaying a full pattern where there are several individual diamond patterns. The basic pattern unit in 'Fairisle' is defined as a square. This is shown in (d). One half of the square 'a' is used to construct the interior of the diamond, and the outside half 'b' defines what becomes the alternating diamond. This is more easily understood by

Individual stitch   Interlocking stitches   Diamond pattern   Pattern unit

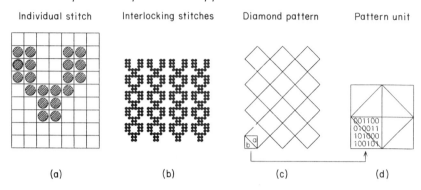

(a)   (b)   (c)   (d)

Fig. 7.5 Stitch and pattern units

examining Plate 24. The '0's and '1's are whatever colours the user desires and comprise all the data required to form a complete pattern. The program flips 'a' and 'b' over horizontally, vertically and diagonally so that the square containing the entire diamond is filled with a geometric pattern.

Once the pattern is determined the program can be used interactively to try out various colour schemes, but first a table of colours must be provided. This table contains a complete definition of all the wool colours that the user has available. To facilitate matching a wool colour to one understood by the computer Fairisle includes a colour mixing routine. Figure 7.6 illustrates one of the mechanisms available in this routine. Either of two colour triangles are displayed; the one depicted in Fig. 7.6 is RGB based. It has pure red at the top and green and blue on the base corners. In the display used to generate the colour plates 16 colours can be displayed simultaneously from a palette of 4096 possible colours. This is because each of the primaries (red, green and blue) has 16 levels of intensity, giving $16 \times 16 \times 16$ (4096) permutations. In Fig. 7.6 the RGB intensity values of each circle are given. The program calculates a reasonable series of steps between the colour codes at each apex of the triangle. This gives a good initial selection of colours. The user then has a series of controls to track down the shade most closely approximating the wool colour. These include increasing or decreasing the colour circles by one level of red, green or blue. Of the other controls the one illustrated in Fig. 7.6 allows the user to select one set of circles and display a new triangle with those circles at the apices (in this example 5, 8 and 9). The second initial triangle begins with the complementary colours (cyan, magenta, and yellow) at each apex. This is illustrated in Plate 24 together with a triangle of closely related shades in Plate 25. Whenever a colour shade is mixed satisfactorily it is stored in a data file until a complete library of wool colours is completed. These can then be accessed by the pattern display.

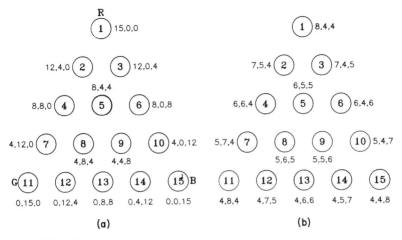

Fig. 7.6 Fairisle colour mixing

Once a set of colours has been chosen the colour codes in the pattern can be changed to duplicate these codes. The user now simply cycles through these until a satisfactory colour scheme is arrived at. Plate 23 shows a second colour scheme for the same pattern.

Fairisle is a short, easy to use program which could be used on any terminal or home computer capable of displaying a reasonable number of colours. Its entire objective was to help visualize different colour schemes for jerseys before knitting them. This it accomplishes neatly and efficiently. It demonstrates the potential of any size of computer to aid in exploring interesting and useful ideas and designs.

7.5 PROJECTS

1. Write a program that can imitate your own handwriting. This will require careful analysis of how you produce each individual character and how you normally join them together. Remember to make the data defining the characters as compact as possible (see Appendix 2).
2. Select some concept that you think is difficult to grasp and that can be explained more easily using computer graphics (e.g. a mathematical or economic 'law'). Write an easy to understand CAL program (using graphics) to explain this concept.
3. Select a board game that you think could be implemented on a small computer. Try to produce a visual simulation as close to the original as possible, including animation effects such as moving counters and rolling dice. A few possibilities might be Scrabble, Snakes and Ladders, Monopoly and Ludo.

4. Are there any forms of domestic handicraft that you think are suitable for a home computer? Try to write a program that helps in the design stage of such a handicraft (e.g. a patchwork quilt or kitchen tile design).

Appendix 1

Pascal examples

The following function calculates the light intensity falling over a planar surface due to a light source at position S (a 3-D point). It requires the following arguments:

P1, P2, P3   Three non-collinear points lying on the polygon

S   The X, Y, Z position of the light source

INTEN   Intensity of the light source

The routine as written below will give inaccurate results if the light source is very close to the planar surface. A practical (if inelegant) solution to this is to put a ceiling on the value of Bright.

```
program bright;

Type          Point = array [1..3] of real;

function
              Bright (P1, P2, P3, S: point; Intens: real): real;

var
              Vect_p1_p2,
              Vect_p2_p3,
              Vect_p1_S,
              Normal                              : point;
              distance,
              Norm_len      : real;
              i             : integer;
              Result        : real;

begin
(*Calculate the vectors lying in the plane and one to the light source ...*)
```

```
for i : = 1 to 3 do
          begin
          Vect_p1_p2 [i] := P2[i] −P1[i];
          Vect_p2_p3[i] := P3[i] −P2[i];
          Vect_p1_S[i] := S[i] −P[i]
          end;
```

(* Calculate normal vector to the surface using vector cross product
Vect_p1_p2 × Vect_p2_p3 *)

```
Normal [1] : = Vect_p1_p2[1]*Vect_p2_p3[2] −
              Vect_p1_p2[2]*Vect_p2_p3[1];

Normal [2] : = Vect_p1_p2[3]*Vect_p2_p3[1] −
              Vect_p1_p2[1]*Vect_p2_p3[3];

Normal [3] : = Vect_p1_p2[2]*Vect_p2_p3[3] −
              Vect_p1_p2[3]*Vect_p2_p3[2];
```

(* Calculate distance from P1 to light source *)

```
distance := sqrt ( Vect_p1_S[1]*Vect_p1_S[1] +
                   Vect_p1_S[2]*Vect_p1_S[2] +
                   Vect_p1_S[3]*Vect_p1_S[3] );
```

(* and the length of the Normal vector *)

```
Norm_len := sqrt (Normal[1]*Normal[1] +
                  Normal[2]*Normal[2] +
                  Normal[3]*Normal[3] );
```

(* And finally the brightness *)

(* Calculate the dot product Normal.Vect_p1_S *)

```
Result := Normal[1]*Vect_p1_S[1] +
          Normal[2]*Vect_p1_S[2] +
          Normal[3]*Vect_p1_S[3];
```

(* and the cosine of the angle between them *)

```
Result := Result / (distance * Norm_len);
```

(* and now the result *)

```
Bright := Result * Intens / (distance*distance);

end;                                    (* function Bright *)

begin
end.
```

Appendix 2

Vector typography

For most of the 1960s and 70s the only text writing facilities available at many installations were very primitive characters made up of a few simple vectors. These characters tended to comprise the ASCII character set plus a few miscellaneous symbols. Besides each character being very crude they were almost invariably monospaced (e.g. an 'i' took up the same width as did a much wider character such as a 'w') resulting in a very artificial and unnatural appearance when plotted. Figure A2.1 is an illustration of a typical set of these characters.

Although many software packages offered more professional looking and controllable character sets it wasn't until the beginning of the 80s that many sites acquired these improved character sets for themselves. These improved systems offered several advantages over the types shown in Fig. A2.1. They usually included Greek characters (useful for scientific and mathematical graphs), italic fonts and serif fonts (serifs are short, normally horizontal strokes added to the main stroke of a character). In addition to this greater range of character types such text systems also provided proportional spacing, producing a more flexible and readable end result. A range of these character sets, using proportional spacing, is shown in Fig. A2.2.

Probably the most irritating problem with both the types of text discussed above is that they do not get any thicker when enlarged. To overcome this problem several solutions have been suggested which centre on repeatedly drawing the character in slightly different positions to give it a solid appearance. One of the most elegant, and effective, algorithms to improve even the most basic font is to use the circumference of a circle to generate a series of

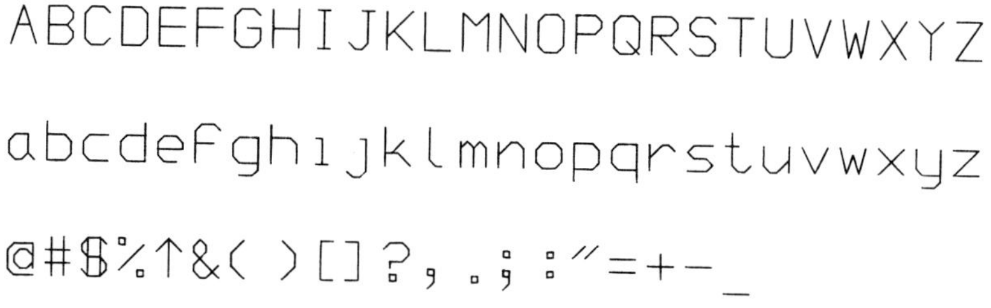

ABCDEFGHIJKLMNOPQRSTUVWXYZ

abcdefghijklmnopqrstuvwxyz

@#$%↑&( )[] ? , . ; : " = + − _

Fig. A2.1 Primitive character set

Simple font with no serifs

Thickened font with serifs

Thickened, unjoined italic

Simple joined Italic

𝕲𝖔𝖙𝖍𝖎𝖈 𝕰𝖓𝖌𝖑𝖎𝖘𝖍 𝖋𝖔𝖓𝖙

Fig. A2.2 Range showing improved character set

starting points to draw the character. The thickness of the character can be controlled by varying the size of the circle, and the density of the character can be controlled by varying the number of points around the circle from which it is drawn. Figure A2.3 shows this algorithm a little more clearly. The pseudo-code below is a simple routine to generate a sequence of these starting positions. It only requires an initial (X, Y) position for the text, and the string of text itself. The other parameters specify the width of the radius, the starting and finishing angle, and the number of steps to be computed. Figure A2.4 is a set of examples produced by varying these parameters.

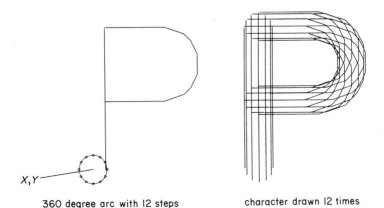

360 degree arc with 12 steps   character drawn 12 times

Fig. A2.3 Circumference algorithm

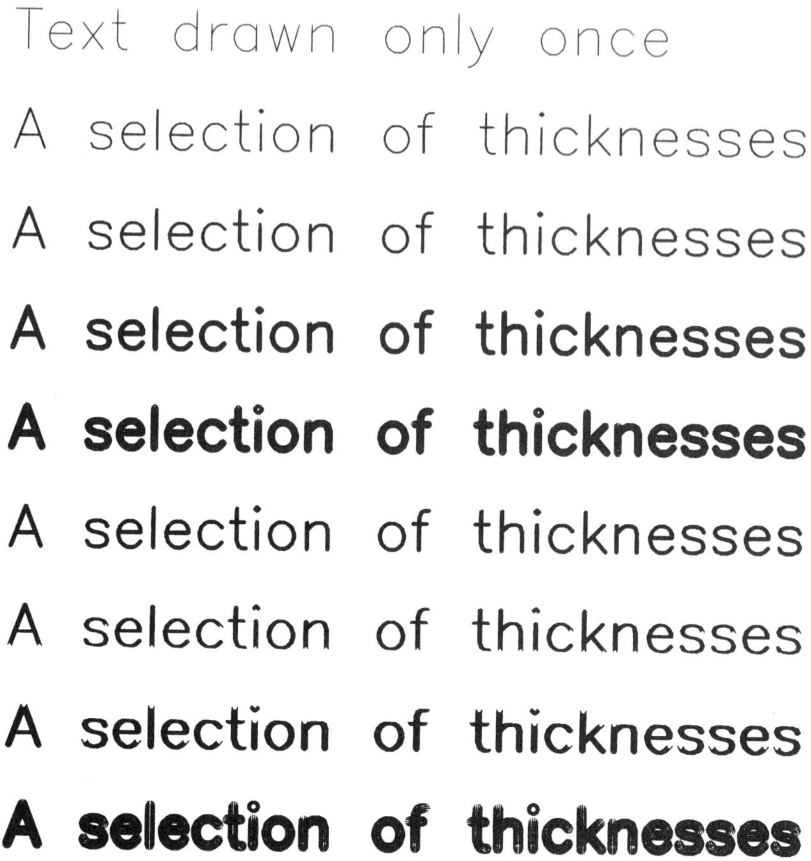

Text drawn only once

A selection of thicknesses

A selection of thicknesses

A selection of thicknesses

A **selection** of **thicknesses**

A selection of thicknesses

A selection of thicknesses

A selection of thicknesses

A **selection** of **thicknesses**

Fig. A2.4 Circumference examples

Routine THICKEN (X,Y,String, radius, theta, phi, steps)

X,Y	:Initial starting position of text string
String	:Characters to be drawn
Radius	:Radius of circle (or arc)
Theta	:Starting angle of arc
Phi	:Number of degrees in arc (360 = a circle)
Steps	:Number of individual steps on arc
Range	= PHI−THETA (size of arc)
SLICE	= STEPS−1 (number of steps)
SEGMENT	= RANGE/SLICE (individual step)

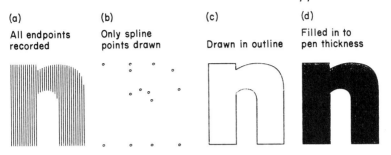

(a)
All endpoints
recorded

(b)
Only spline
points drawn

(c)
Drawn in outline

(d)
Filled in to
pen thickness

Fig. A2.5 Endpoints and splines

```
for j :        = 1 to steps do begin
ANGLE          = Theta + Segment * j
XNEW           = X + Radius * (cosine of ANGLE)
YNEW           = Y + Radius * (sine of ANGLE)
Draw text beginning at (XNEW,YNEW)
end
```

A totally different method of defining and storing characters is being adopted by several installations because of the flexibility it offers. In digital typesetting environments one system of specifying text is to record the end points of a series of vertical lines which together form an individual character. Example (a) in Fig. A2.5 illustrates this technique. Its main attraction is that when the character is expanded proportionally more points (and therefore lines) can be interpolated between the original end points. An extension of this principle requires even fewer points to generate good quality characters. In (b) only the end points of a few straight lines plus four spline points need to be stored. Using these the computer can draw the outside straight lines and fit a curve through the spline points to produce a smooth looking character (c). A further advantage is that a sequence of lines within a character can then be computed to shade it in (d).

Obviously complex characters (e.g. '&') and very curvy fonts require more spline points (and more time to design) but this technique is still very useful for producing outline and shaded characters on plotters and raster displays.

Appendix 3

The computer and colour

Colour is the single most valuable key in appreciating and responding to the visual world around us. It gives shape and form, solidity and depth to every object we see, and yet it remains one of the most subjective of all our senses. To translate the colours of the everyday world into a form suitable for manipulation by computer is one of the most sensitive and difficult tasks facing computer graphics. The huge growth in raster type terminals seems certain to result in colour graphic displays becoming the normal, so effective methods of understanding and specifying colours are essential.

The human eye is a machine delicately tuned to various wavelengths of light. These wavelengths create the impressions that we name colours. Short wavelengths cause a blue sensation, middle wavelengths a green sensation, and long wavelengths a red sensation. Although there are seven hues in the visible part of the light spectrum an almost infinite number of colour variations can be produced by mixing different intensities of red, green and blue light (known as 'primaries'). When light of all visible wavelengths is present we are able to perceive colour in objects, this is because their surface pigments absorb some wavelengths but reflect others. Thus a blade of grass appears green because it contains pigments that reflect only green wavelengths. The intensity of the green reflected depends upon the strength of the light and the shininess of the surface pigment. Understanding how graphic displays reproduce colour is the first step towards defining a method of specifying the exact colour we want displayed.

The first chapter of this book touched upon the mechanism by which different colours can be made to appear on a raster display. Figure A3.1(a) shows how the three primaries red, green and blue can be mixed together to form their complementaries cyan, magenta and yellow. Adding all three primaries together forms white, none at all results in pure black. Extending this process to a video display is straightforward. Each pixel on a t.v. or raster display is composed of three phosphors (red, green and blue) placed very close to each other. Though these phosphors do not actually touch they are so small that the eye fuses them together to form one colour. Switching off or on various combinations of these phosphors produce the colours shown in Fig. A3.1(b). These eight colours are common to many graphic terminals, particularly when driven by a microcomputer. The reason for this is that only one piece of infor-

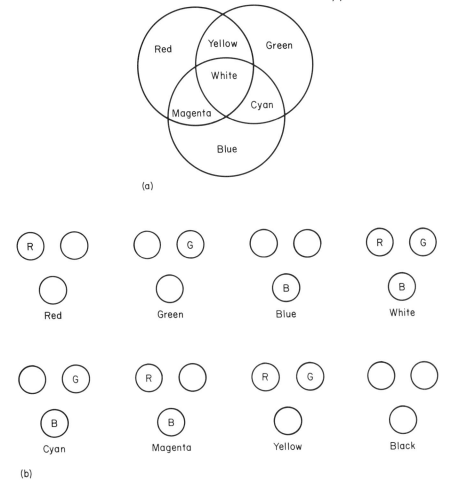

Fig. A3.1 Colour mixing

mation need be stored for each phosphor in a pixel, that is whether it is on or off. To display more colours than these basic eight requires additional information to control the intensity of the red, green and blue electron guns. The more information that can be stored concerning these phosphors the more colours can be displayed. The amount of information controlling each colour gun is provided by memory boards inside a controller which is housed either inside the colour terminal or in an external 'black box'. Many of these controllers can store sufficient data to specify 256 discrete levels of intensity for each phosphor. This gives a possible range of 256 × 256 × 256 or 16.2 million colours. The only problem in having such a large number of available colours is

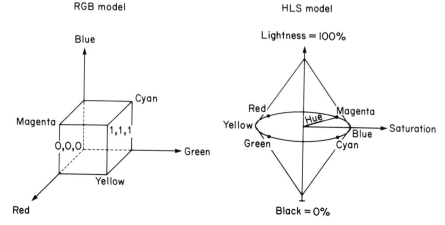

Fig. A3.2 RGB and HLS models

that people cannot easily define a colour in terms of RGB (red,green,blue) values. It is necessary therefore to turn to other methods of defining colours which seem more natural to the way we perceive and think of colour.

Most people are familiar from childhood with mixing paint pigments together to form various colours. The pigment primaries are red, blue and yellow, the secondaries are orange, green and purple. A pure colour (or pigment) is normally defined as being 'fully saturated'. Adding white pigment to it lightens the colour and is known as tinting. Adding black pigment reduces the intensity of the colour and produces shades. Using these very familiar processes as a base a number of colour models have evolved over the years which try to organize all visible colours into a confined 3-D space. Specifying an X, Y and Z location inside this space defines an exact colour. All the various systems agree broadly to three properties of a colour which comprise the three axes:

Hue	Distinguishes the actual wavelength and is what we often mean by the word colour (e.g. red, blue, yellow, green).
Saturation	Also known as intensity or chroma and most directly refers to the purity of the colour, that is how diluted the colour is (e.g. bottle green and lime green, pink and red).
Lightness	Also known as luminance or value and allows the colour to be ranked from black to white.

Figure A3.2 illustrates the RGB model used by most colour graphic displays and a typical HLS (hue, lightness and saturation) model. The HLS model shown interprets colours as coordinates in a double cone. Hue is represented as the angle around the vertical axis and is expressed in degrees. Lightness is 0% at the lower tip (i.e. black) and 100% at the upper tip (i.e. white). Saturation is measured from 0% on the vertical axis to 100% on the outside edge of the cone. This particular model is based on the Ostwald colour system and is widely used by Tektronix.

R	G	B		HUE		
0	0	0	Black	Blue	=	0
1.0	1.0	1.0	White	Magenta	=	60
1.0	0.0	0.0	Red	Red	=	120
1.0	0.2	0.2	Pink	Yellow	=	180
1.0	1.0	0.0	Yellow	Green	=	240
1.0	1.0	0.4	Light Yellow	Cyan	=	300

Specifying a colour in terms of hue, lightness and saturation may be more natural and convenient but requires conversion into RGB coordinates for eventual display. Several of the articles mentioned in the Bibliography (under Colour) go into the problems involved in accomplishing this accurately, and Foley and Van Dam (see introduction to Bibliography) provide the code to perform the necessary translation from one system to the other.

PROBLEMS AND GUIDELINES IN COLOUR USAGE

The most frustrating property of colour is that it will change radically when viewed under different conditions. As objects recede away from a viewer the density of the atmosphere will tend to reduce contrasts and mute any strong colours. Objects a long way away (such as mountains) appear to become bluish. Apparent changes in colour are especially striking when a colour is surrounded by different colours. For instance, if one specific shade of red is placed next to yellow it will appear bluer, next to blue it will appear yellower, next to green it becomes brighter and stronger. Black will make it darker and white will brighten and lighten it. Colours generally deepen when surrounded by different, lighter colours. Proceeding from this it is possible to provide a few simple guidelines when using colour.

1. Blue and green are passive and work well as histogram bars and pie chart segments.
2. Red and yellow are much stronger and dynamic, this makes them ideal to direct attention to specific points of interest. This might be a particular pie segment, curve, or histogram bar.
3. Polygons can be given more emphasis and interest when their edge is picked out by some pure, warm colour (e.g. red).
4. Dark colours on a black background (e.g. blue on black) or light colours on a white background (e.g. yellow or cyan on white) provide very poor contrast and will just become lost.

5. Colours similar in hue, lightness or saturation will convey less contrast and are consequently very easy on the eye.
6. Colours differing greatly in hue, lightness or saturation provide sharp contrast when placed near each other.
7. Striking, effective charts and pictures can be produced by using just one strong colour (in moderation) on top of a complementary background.

Bibliography

Every year sees a huge increase in the amount of literature dealing with various aspects of computer graphics: keeping up to date with all this new information can be a time-consuming occupation so a more selective diet is recommended. To help in choosing your own particular diet the books and articles detailed in the following pages include general works concerned with the subject matter of each chapter, plus recent articles on some of the more interesting current areas of research. To anyone already familiar with computer graphics two books may be conspicuous by their absence, namely:

1. Foley, J.D. and Van Dam, A. (1982) *Fundamentals of Interactive Computer Graphics*, Addison-Wesley, Reading, Mass.
2. Newman, W.M. and Sproull, R.F., (1979) *Principles of Interactive Graphics*, 2nd Edn, McGraw-Hill, New York.

The reason is that both books deserve emphasizing in that they offer a thorough examination of computer graphics, particularly interactive graphics, and contain exhaustive bibliographies. In effect they have become a kind of *de facto* standard of required reading to anyone desiring a complete grounding in the subject. The Foley and Van Dam book is especially useful to anyone wishing to write Core-compatible software.

To try to keep abreast of developments (almost as they happen) four journals are of especial value:

Computer Graphics (sponsored by the ACM)
Computer Graphics and Applications (IEEE publication)
ACM Transactions on Graphics
Computer Graphics Forum (Eurographics Journal, North Holland, Amsterdam)

HARDWARE

Baxter, B. (1981) Three-dimensional display viewing device for examining internal structure. *Proc. Soc. Photo-Opt. Instrum. Eng*, **283**, 111–5.
Clark, D.R. (ed.) (1981) *The Computer Image*, Pergamon Press, Oxford.
Fuchs, H., Pizer, S.M. Tsai, L.C. Bloomberg, S.H. and Heinz, E.R. (1982) Adding a true 3-D display to a raster graphics system. *IEEE Comput. Graphics Appl.,*, **2**, No. 7, 73–8.
Lazik, G.L. (1976) A three-dimensional display with true depth and parallax. *Proc. 1976 Soc. Inf. Disp. Int. Symp.* **May**, 105.

Lerner, E.J. (1981) The computer graphics revolution. *IEEE Spectrum*, **18**, No. 2, Feb., 35—9.

Lucido, A.P. (1978) An overview of directed beam graphics display hardware. *Computer*, **11**, Nov., 29—36.

Machover, C. (1977) CRT graphic terminals. *Comput. Graphics Art*, **2**, No. 2, May, 16—29.

McEwing, R.W. (1977) Touch displays in industrial computer systems. *Displays for Man—Machine Systems*, IEEE Publ. No. 150, 79—81.

Page, C.J. Pugh, A. and Heginbotham, W.B. (1976) New technique for tactile imaging. *Radio Electron. Eng.*, **Nov.**, 519—26.

Permutter, R.J. and Friedland, S.S. (1983) Computer-generated holograms in biology and medicine. *IEEE Comput. Graphics Appl.*, **3**, No. 5, 47—52.

Pleshko, P. (1982) AC plasma flat panel displays. *Comput. Graphics World*, **5**, No. 7, July, 47—8.

Preiss, R. (1978) Storage CRT display terminals: evolution and trends. *Computer*, **11**, No. 11, Nov., 20—6.

Schmandt, C. (1983) Spatial input/display correspondence in a stereoscopic computer graphic work station. *Comput. Graphics*, **17**, No. 3, July, 253—63.

Sherr, S. (1982) *Video and Digital Electronic Displays — A User's Guide*, John Wiley, New York.

Tannas, L. (1978) Flat panel displays in perspective. *Proc. Soc. Inf. Disp.*, **19**, No. 4, 193—8.

Whieldon, D. (1981) The newest CRTs: graphics and more. *Comput. Decisions*, **Aug.**

2-D SOFTWARE

Blinn, J.F. and Newell, M.E. (1978) Clipping using homogeneous coordinates. *Comput. Graphics*, **12**, Aug., 245—51.

Bresenham, J. (1977) A linear algorithm for incremental digital display of circular arcs. *Commun. ACM*, **20**, Feb., 100—6.

Cyrus, M. and Beck, J. (1978) Generalized two- and three-dimensional clipping. *Comput. Graphics*, **3**, 23—8.

Earnshaw, R.A. (1977) Line generation for incremental and raster devices. *Comput. Graphics*, **11**, Summer, 199—205.

Giloi, W.K. (1978) *Interactive Computer Graphics*, Prentice-Hall, Englewood Cliffs, N.J.

Hatfield, L. and Herzog, B. (1982) Graphics software-from techniques to principles. *IEEE Comput. Graphics Appl.*, **2**, No. 1. 59—76.

Pal, T.K. (1978) Intrinsic spline curve with local control. *Comput. Aided Design*, **10**, Jan. 19—29.

Pavlidis, T. (1978) Filling algorithms for raster graphics. *Comput. Graphics*, **12**, Aug., 161—6.

Pavlidis, T. (1982) *Algorithms for Graphics and Image Processing*, Computer Science Press, New York.

Pitteway, M. and Watkinson, D. (1980) Bresenham's algorithm with grey scale. *Commun. ACM*, **23**, No. 11, Nov., 625—6.

Sutherland, I.E. and Hodgman, G.W. (1974) Reentrant polygon clipping. *Commun. ACM*, **17**, No. 1, Jan. 32—42.

Whitted, T. (1983) Anti-aliased line drawing using brush extrusion. *Comput. Graphics*, **17**, No. 3, July, 151—7.

3-D SOFTWARE

Blinn, J.F. (1978), *Computer Display of Curved Surfaces*, PhD Dissertation, University of Utah.

Blinn, J.F. (1982) Light reflection functions for simulation of clouds and dusty surfaces. *Proc. SIGGRAPH 1982.*

Catmull, E. (1978) A hidden-surface algorithm, with anti-aliasing. *Comput. Graphics*, **12**, Aug., 6—11.

Cook, R.L. and Torrance, K. (1981) A reflectance model for computer graphics, Proc. SIGGRAPH

1981. *Comput. Graphics,* **15**, No. 3, Aug., 307—16.

Crow, F. (1977) Shadow algorithms for computer graphics. *Comput. Graphics,* **11**, No. 2, Summer 242—7.

Etra, B. and Katz, L. (1977) Inexpensive real-time imageneration and control. *Comput. Graphics,* **11**, Sprint, 41—6.

Mandelbrot, B. (1982) *The Fractal Geometry of Nature,* W.H. Freeman, San Francisco, Calif.

Myers, W. (1979) Interactive computer graphics: flying high — Part II. *Computer,* **12**, No. 8, Aug., 52—67.

Norton, A. (1982) Generation and display of geometric fractals in 3-D. *Proc. SIGGRAPH 1982. Comput. Graphics* (US), **July**, 61—7.

Phong, Bui-Tuong, Illumination for computer generated images. *Commun. ACM,* **18**, June, 311—7.

Requicha, A.A.G and Voelcker, H.B. (1982) Solid modelling: A historical summary and contemporary assessment. *IEEE Comput. Graphics Appl.,* **Mar.**

Roese, J. and McCleary, L. (1979) Steroscopic computer graphics for simulation and modelling, Proc. SIGGRAPH 1979. *Comput. Graphics,* **13**, No. 2, Aug., 41—7.

Schweitzer, D. (1983) Artificial texturing: an aid to surface visualisation. *Comput. Graphics,* **17**, No. 3, July, 23—31.

Warn, D.R. (1983) Lighting controls for synthetic images. *Comput. Graphics,* **17**, No. 3, July, 13—23.

SOFTWARE STANDARDS, CORE AND GKS

ANSI X3H3 Computer Graphics Standards Committee (1982) *American National Standard Functional Specification of the Programmer's Minimal Interface for Graphics,* American National Standards Institute document X3H3/82-15rl, Feb.

Bergeron, R.D., Bono, P.R. and Foley, J.D. (1978) Graphics programming using the Core System. *Comput. Surv.,* **10**, No. 4, Dec., 389—443.

Bono, P.R., Encarnacao, J.L., Hopgood, F.R.A. and Ten Hagen, P. (1982) GKS — the first graphics standard. *IEEE Comput. Graphics Appl.,* **2**, No. 5, 9—23.

Carson, G.S. (1983) The specification of computer graphics systems. *IEEE Comput. Graphics Appl.,* **3**, No. 6, 27—43.

Encarnacao, J., Enderle, G., Kansy, K., Nees, G., Schlechtendahl, Weiss, J. and Wisskirchen, (1980) The workstation concepts of GKS and the resulting conceptual differences to the GSPC core system. *Proc. SIGGRAPH 1980. Comput. Graphics,* **14**, No. 3, July, 226—30.

Hopgood, F.R.A., Duce, D.A., Gallop, J.R. and Sutcliffe, D.C. (1983) *Introduction to the Graphical Kernel System (GKS),* Academic Press, London.

International Standards Organisation (1982) *Graphical Kernel System (GKS), Version 7.2,* International Standards Organisation.

Lerman, K. (1981) *Suggested Outline for GKS Standard,* American National Standards Institute document X3H34/81-1, Jan.

Rosenthal, D.S.H. (1980) *A Framework for Specifying GKS,* American National Standards Institute document X3H3/80-63.

Rosenthal, D.S.H., Michener, J.C., Pfaff, G., Kessener, R. and Sabin, M. (1982) The detailed semantics of graphics input devices. *Comput. Graphics,* **16**, No. 3, 33—8.

Special Issue: Graphics Standards (1978) *Comput. Surv.* , **10**, No. 4.

Sutcliffe, D.C. (1982) Attribute handling in GKS. *Eurographics,* 103—10.

INDUSTRIAL APPLICATIONS

Chasen, S.H. (1978) *Geometric Principles and Procedures for Computer Graphics Applications,* Prentice-Hall, Englewood Cliffs, N.J.

Fraser, D.R. (1980) *The Computer in Contemporary Cartography*, John Wiley, New York.

Gust, R.K. (1983) Designing effective business graphics. *IEEE Comput. Graphics Appl.*, **3**, No. 4, 33—8.

Head, R.W. (1972) *Manager's Guide to Management Information Systems*, Prentice-Hall, Englewood Cliffs, N.J.

IEEE Comput. Graphics Appl. (1982) **2**, No. 2. Entire issue devoted to solid modelling.

Laurie, J.R. (1973) *Textile Graphics/Computer-Aided*, Fairchild Books and Visuals, New York.

Leray, P. (1982) The CIG system of synthetic image generation. *IEEE Comput. Graphics Appl.*, **2**, No. 5, 89—92.

Machover, C. (1982) Unlimited potential — business graphics. *Computerworld OA*, **Dec.**, 51—4.

Machover, C. and Blauth, R. (1980) *The CAD/CAM Handbook*, Computervision Corp, Bedford.

Max, N.L. (1983) Computer representation of molecular surfaces. *IEEE Comput. Graphics Appl.*, **3**, No. 5, 21—30.

Morris, J.G. (1979) Using color in industrial control graphics. *Control Eng.*, **26**, No. 7, July, 41—5.

Negroponte, N. (ed.) (1975) *Computer Aids to Design and Architecture*, Petrocelli-Charter, New York.

Prince, M.D. (1971) *Interactive Graphics for Computer-Aided Design*, Addison-Wesley, Reading, Mass.

Ryan, R.L. (1979) *Computer-Aided Graphics and Design*, Marcel Dekker, New York.

Schachter, B.J. (ed.) (1983) *Computer Image Generation*, Wiley—Interscience, New York.

Shimomura, T. (1983) A method for automatically generating business graphs, *IEEE Comput. Graphics Appl.*, **3**, No. 6, 55—60.

ART AND ANIMATION

Badler, N.I. and Smoliar, S.W. (1979) Digital representations of human movement. *Comput. Surv.*, **11**, No. 1, Mar., 19—38.

Beach, R., and Stone, M. (1983) Graphical style — towards high quality illustrations. *Comput. Graphics*, **17**, No. 3, July 127—35.

Brassel, K.E. and Utano, J.J. (1978) Font variation in vector plotter lettering. *Comput. Graphics*, **11**, Mar., 67—77.

Brown, M.D. and Smoliar, S.W. (1978) Preparing dance notation scores with a computer. *Comput. Graphics*, **3**, No. 1, 1—7.

Burtnyk, N. and Wein, M. (1976) Interactive skeleton techniques for enhancing motion dynamics in key frame animation. *Commun. ACM*, **19**, No. 10, **Oct.**

Catmull, E. (1978) The problems of computer-assisted animation, Proc. SIGGRAPH 1978. *Comput. Graphics*, **12**, No. 3, Aug., 348—53.

Crow, F.C. (1978) The use of grey scale for improved raster display of vectors and characters. *Comput. Graphics*, **12**, Aug., 1—5.

Dietrich, F. and Molnar, Z. (1981) Pictures by funny numbers. *Creative Computing*, **7**, No. 6, 102—7.

Feiner, S., Salesin, D. and Banchoff, T. (1982) Dial: A diagrammatic animation language. *IEEE Comput. Graphics Appl.*, **2**, No. 7, 43—56.

Hackathorn, R.J. (1977) ANIMA II, a 3-D color animation system, Proc. SIGGRAPH 1977. *Comput. Graphics*, **11**, No. 2, Summer, 54—64.

Hertlein, G.C. (1977) Computer art for computer people — a syllabus. *Comput. Graphics*, **11**, No. 2, Summer, 249—54.

IEEE Comput. Graphics Appl., (1982) **2**, No. 9, Entire issue devoted to Human Body Models and Animation.

Kitching, A. (1973) Computer animation — some new ANTICS. *Br. Kinematogr. Sound Telev.*, **55**, No. 12, Dec. 372—86.

Knowlton, K. (1981) Computer-aided definition, manipulation, and depiction of objects composed of spheres. *Comput. Graphics*, **15**, No. 2, Apr., 48–71.
Korein, J. and Badler, N. (1983) Temporal anti-aliasing in computer generated animation. *Comput. Graphics*, **17**, No. 3, July, 377–89.
Madsen, R. (1969) *Animated Film: Concepts, Methods, Uses*, Interland, New York.
Marcus, A. (1980) Computer-assisted chart making from the graphic designer's perspective. *Comput. Graphics*, **14**, No. 3, 247–53.
Marcus, A. (1982) Typographics design for interfaces of information systems, *Proc. Human Factors in Computer Systems*, National Bureau of Standards, pp. 26–30.
Marcus, A. (1983) Graphic design for computer graphics. *IEEE Comput. Graphics Appl.*, **3**, No. 4, 63–70.
Menosky, J. (1982) Video graphics and grand jetes: choreography by computer. *Science*, **3**, No. 4, May, 24–33.
Palyka, D. (1982) Artistic reflections on man–machine interfaces. *Proc. Graphics Interface 1982 Conf., Toronto*, pp. 291–3.
Parke, F.I. (1972) A parametric model for human faces. *Proc. ACM Nat. Conf.*, **1**, Aug., 451–7.
Parke, F.I. (1975) A model for human faces that allows speech synchronized animation. *J. Comput. Graphics*, **1**, No. 1, Mar., 1–4.
Platt, S.M. and Badler, N.I. (1981) Animating facial expressions, Proc. SIGGRAPH 1981. *Comput. Graphics*, **15**, No. 3, Aug., 245–52.
Reeves, W.T. (1981) Inbetweening for computer animation utilizing moving point constraints. *Comput. Graphics*, **15**, No. 3, Aug., 263–9.
Reichardt, J. (1971) *The Computer and Art*, Van Nostrand Reinhold, Wokingham.
Reynolds, C.W. (1982) Computer animation with scripts and actors, Proc. SIGGRAPH 1982. *Comput. Graphics*, **16**, No. 3, July, 289–96.
Weber, L., Smoliar, S.W. and Badler, N.I. (1978) An architecture for the simulation of human movement. *Proc. ACM 1978 Ann. Conf., Washington, D.C.*, **Dec.**, pp. 737–45.
Willmert, K.D. (1978) Graphic display of human motion, *Proc. ACM 1978 Ann. Conf., Washington, D.C.*, **Dec.**, pp. 715–9.
Zeltzer, D. (1982) Representation of complex animated figures. *Proc. Graphics Interface 1982 Conf., Toronto*, pp. 205–11.

COLOUR

Agoston, G.A. (1979) *Colour Theory and Its Application in Art and Design*, Springer-Verlag, Berlin.
Hiskey, H.D. (1978) The colors of computing. *Computer*, **11**, May, 8–9.
Hunt, R.W.G. (1975) *The Reproduction of Colour*, 3rd edn, John Wiley, New York.
Joblove, G.H. and Greenberg, D. (1978) Color spaces for computer graphics. *Comput. Graphics*, **12**, Aug., 20–25.
Marcus, A. (1982) Colour: a tool for computer graphics communication in *The Computer Image*, Addison-Wesley, Reading, Mass., pp. 76–90.
Smith, A.R. (1978) Color gamut transform pairs. *Comput. Graphics*, **12**, Aug., 12–19.
Wyszecki, G. and Stiles, W.S. (1982) *Color Science*, 2nd edn, John Wiley, New York.

MICROCOMPUTERS

Bechtolsheim, A. and Baskett, F. (1980) High-performance raster graphics for microcomputer systems, Proc. SIGGRAPH 1980, *Comput. Graphics*, **14**, No. 3, July, 43–7.
Seaman, J. (1981) Microcomputers in the executive suite. *Computer Decisions*, **Feb.**

Index